50 Years of
PRESERVED STEAM
on the
MAIN LINE

On 17th March 1984 No. 5051 *Drysllwyn Castle* struggles towards the summit at Llanvihangel with a southbound "Welsh Marches Express".

John Whiteley

50 Years of
PRESERVED STEAM
on the
MAIN LINE

J. S. Whiteley & G. W. Morrison

Haynes

Oxford Publishing Co.

A FOULIS-OPC Railway Book

Published by:
Haynes Publishing Group
Sparkford, Near Yeovil, Somerset. BA22 7JJ

Haynes Publications Inc.
861 Lawrence Drive, Newbury Park, California 91320, USA.

Printed by J.H. Haynes & Co.

British Library Cataloguing in Publication Data
Whiteley, J.S. (John Stuart), 1943–
  50 years of preserved steam on the main line.
  1. Great Britain. Preserved steam locomotives, 1971–1982
  I. Title   II. Morrison, Gavin W. (Gavin Wedderburn), 1936–

  625.2'61'0941
  ISBN .i.0-86093-432-2

Library of Congress Catalog Card Number
89-84715

Title page: The start of it all. GNR No. 1 on 24th August 1938 when it ran from King's Cross to Cambridge, where depicted. The seven coaches were reconditioned specially for the specials to show the public what a typical train of East Coast Joint stock was like in the 1890s.

Contents

Introduction

August 1968 witnessed the end of steam traction on British Railways, and although a few preserved steam locomotives had worked on the lines of BR prior to that date, it was inconceivable then that such a renaissance would happen during the next twenty years. Tribute indeed to the dedication and effort which has been made by a relatively small number of individuals and preservation societies for which the many thousands of enthusiasts and the general public at large owe a huge debt of gratitude. Had this not been the case, steam locomotives would no doubt simply have survived as static museum exhibits. Time and effort alone has not produced the remarkable results which have been achieved, but at times also, a considerable financial investment, and without the co-operation of British Rail it would not have been possible to see main line steam running as it exists today.

Following the elimination of steam traction from the main lines of BR, in August 1968, only No. 4472 *Flying Scotsman* was allowed to run for a short period. However, in October 1971, BR relaxed its main line steam ban following concerted efforts by enthusiasts, preservationists and locomotive owners, and No. 6000 *King George V* was allowed to work a main line train of "Cider Pullmans" from Hereford. A demand for organized steam-hauled tours was quickly identified by both the Steam Locomotive Operators Association and also British Rail and successful excursions have subsequently been run over a number of scenic routes using a variety of locomotives which have been meticulously restored to the exacting mechanical standards demanded by BR.

Preservation of any kind is an on-going thing, and the preservation and restoration of steam locomotives to running condition is no exception. Although hardly a year goes by nowadays without at least one additional locomotive to the ranks of those passed for main line operation, a number that have seen use in the past are currently out of action or restricted from running on BR metals. The first preserved steam locomotive permitted to run on the main line was the historic occasion when Great Northern Railway No.1 worked a number of specials in 1938. Now, 50 years later there is an ambitious project by the North Eastern Locomotive Preservation Group to restore Peppercorn A2 class Pacific No. 60532 *Blue Peter*. It is already well under way at ICI Wilton and it seems quite conceivable that this fine locomotive will be in steam once again during 1989. With various other schemes in the pipeline, not least of all the intention of the Bluebell Railway to construct a new LBSCR Marsh Atlantic, using an almost indentical Ivatt GNR boiler which has been obtained, it seems that we still have a remarkable variety of preserved steam locomotives to see on the main line in the years to come.

In this book we have attempted to illustrate as comprehensively as possible the wide variety of preserved locomotives that have worked trains on the *main lines*. On the whole, locomotives hauling public fare-paying trains are shown, and a deliberate attempt has been made to exclude pictures of the various engine movements which have taken place in connection with exhibitions and celebrations over the years. The choice of photographs has been extremely difficult and I would like to offer my grateful thanks to fellow photographers who have kindly allowed me to use their pictures, and whose assistance has hopefully helped produce an interesting and balanced selection.

J. S. Whiteley
Shipley, Yorks

In the early days of preservation *Sir Nigel Gresley* heads out of Leeds for Carlisle past Wortley Junction on 1st October 1967.
Gavin Morrison

Summary of Preserved Steam Locomotives that have worked on the Main Line (1938–1988)

Present No.	BR No.	BR 'TOPS' No.	Name	Class	Wheel Arrangement	Builder & Works/Builder's No.	Date Built	Designer	Railway of origin
3440	—	98240	City of Truro	3700 City	4-4-0	GWR Swindon 2000	1903	Dean/Churchward	GWR
2857	2857	98857		2800	2-8-0	GWR Swindon 2763	1918	Churchward	GWR
4555	4555	98455		4500	2-6-2T	GWR Swindon	1924	Churchward	GWR
4079	4079	—	Pendennis Castle	4073 Castle	4-6-0	GWR Swindon	1924	Collett	GWR
5051	5051	98751	Drysllwyn Castle	4073 Castle	4-6-0	GWR Swindon	1936	Collett	GWR
5080	5080	98780	Defiant	4073 Castle	4-6-0	GWR Swindon	1939	Collett	GWR
7029	7029	98729	Clun Castle	4073 Castle	4-6-0	BR Swindon	1950	Collett	BR
4930	4930	98530	Hagley Hall	4900 Hall	4-6-0	GWR Swindon	1929	Collett	GWR
5900	5900	—	Hinderton Hall	4900 Hall	4-6-0	GWR Swindon	1931	Collett	GWR
6000	6000	98800	King George V	6000 King	4-6-0	GWR Swindon	1927	Collett	GWR
6106	6106	—		6100	2-6-2T	GWR Swindon	1931	Collett	GWR
6435	6435	—		6400	0-6-0PT	GWR Swindon	1937	Collett	GWR
1420	1420	—	Bulliver*	1400	0-4-2T	GWR Swindon	1932	Collett	GWR
1466	1466	—		1400	0-4-2T	GWR Swindon	1936	Collett	GWR
7808	7808	—	Cookham Manor	7800 Manor	4-6-0	GWR Swindon	1938	Collett	GWR
7812	7812	98512	Erlestoke Manor	7800 Manor	4-6-0	GWR Swindon	1939	Collett	GWR
7819	7819	98519	Hinton Manor	7800 Manor	4-6-0	GWR Swindon	1939	Collett	GWR
6960	6960	98560	Raveningham Hall	6959 Modified Hall	4-6-0	GWR Swindon	1944	Hawksworth	GWR
6998	6998	98598	Burton Agnes Hall	6959 Modified Hall	4-6-0	BR Swindon	1949	Hawksworth	BR
488	30583	—		0415	4-4-2T	Neilson & Co. 3209	1885	Adams	LSWR
473	32473	—	Birch Grove	E4	0-6-2T	LBSCR Brighton	1898	R. J. Billinton	LBSCR
120	30120	—		T9	4-4-0	LSWR Nine Elms 572	1899	Drummond	LSWR
777	30777	98577	Sir Lamiel	N15 King Arthur	4-6-0	North British 23223	1925	Maunsell	SR
841	30841	98641	Greene King*	S15	4-6-0	SR Eastleigh	1936	Maunsell	SR
850	30850	98750	Lord Nelson	Lord Nelson	4-6-0	SR Eastleigh	1926	Maunsell	SR
35028	35028	98828	Clan Line	Merchant Navy	4-6-2	BR Eastleigh / Rebuilt BR Eastleigh	1948 / 1959	Bulleid	BR
34092	34092	98792	City of Wells	West Country	4-6-2	BR Brighton	1949	Bulleid	BR
123	—	—		"Caledonian Single"	4-2-2	Neilson & Co. 3553	1886	Neilson & Co	CR
790	—	98190	Hardwicke	Precedent	2-4-0	LNWR Crewe 3286	1892	Webb	LNWR
1054	58926	98254		2F	0-6-2T	LNWR Crewe 2979	1888	Webb	LNWR
103	—	—		"Jones Goods"	4-6-0	Sharp, Stewart 4022	1894	Jones	HR
80	41966	—	Thundersley	3P	4-4-2T	R. Stephenson 3367	1909	Whitelegg	LTSR
1000	41000	98400		4P	4-4-0	MR Derby / Rebuilt MR Derby	1902 / Rbt 1914	Johnson (rebuilt Deeley)	MR

53809	53809	98709		7F	2-8-0	R. Stephenson 3895	1925	Fowler	SDJR
6115	6115	98715	Scots Guardsman	Royal Scot	4-6-0	North British 23610; Rebuilt LMSR Crewe	1927; Rbt 1947	Fowler, (rebuilt Stanier)	LMSR
6201	6201	98801	Princess Elizabeth	Princess Royal	4-6-2	LMSR Crewe 107	1933	Stanier	LMSR
5593	5593	98693	Kolhapur	Jubilee	4-6-0	North British 24151	1934	Stanier	LMSR
5596	5596	98696	Bahamas	Jubilee	4-6-0	North British 24154	1935	Stanier	LMSR
5690	5690	98690	Leander	Jubilee	4-6-0	LMSR Crewe 288	1936	Stanier	LMSR
5025	5025	98525		5	4-6-0	Vulcan Foundry 4570	1934	Stanier	LMSR
5000	5000	98500		5	4-6-0	LMSR Crewe 216	1935	Stanier	LMSR
5305	5305	98505	Alderman A. E. Draper*	5	4-6-0	Armstrong Whitworth 1360	1937	Stanier	LMSR
5407	5407	98507		5	4-6-0	Armstrong Whitworth 1462	1937	Stanier	LMSR
44871	44871	98571	Sovereign*	5	4-6-0	LMSR Crewe	1945	Stanier	LMSR
44932	44932	98532		5	4-6-0	LMSR Horwich	1945	Stanier	LMSR
4767	4767	98567	George Stephenson*	5	4-6-0	LMSR Crewe	1947	Stanier	LMSR
48151	48151	98851		8F	2-8-0	LMSR Crewe	1942	Stanier	LMSR
46229	46229	98829	Duchess of Hamilton	Princess Coronation	4-6-2	LMSR Crewe	1938	Stanier	LMSR
46443	46443	98243		2MT	2-6-0	BR Crewe	1950	H. G. Ivatt	BR
43106	43106	98406		4MT	2-6-0	BR Darlington 2148	1951	H. G. Ivatt	BR
1	—	—		"Eight-Foot Single"	4-2-2	GNR Doncaster 50	1870	Stirling	GNR
673	65243	98273	Maude	J36	0-6-0	Neilson & Co. 4392	1891	Holmes	NBR
1247	68846	—		J52	0-6-0ST	Sharp Stewart 4492	1899	H. A. Ivatt	GNR
990	—	—	Henry Oakley	C2	4-4-2	GNR Doncaster 762	1898	H. A. Ivatt	GNR
251	—	—		C1	4-4-2	GNR Doncaster 991	1902	H. A. Ivatt	GNR
256	62469	—	Glen Douglas	D34	4-4-0	NBR Cowlairs	1913	Reid	NBR
49	62277	—	Gordon Highlander	D40	4-4-0	North British 22563	1920	Heywood	GNSR
4472	60103	98872	Flying Scotsman	A3	4-6-2	LNER Doncaster 1564	1923	Gresley	LNER
246	62712	—	Morayshire	D49	4-4-0	LNER Darlington 1391	1928	Gresley	LNER
60009	60009	98809	Union of South Africa	A4	4-6-2	LNER Doncaster 1853	1937	Gresley	LNER
4498	60007	98898	Sir Nigel Gresley	A4	4-6-2	LNER Doncaster 1863	1937	Gresley	LNER
19	60019	—	Bittern	A4	4-6-2	LNER Doncaster 1866	1937	Gresley	LNER
4468	60022	98868	Mallard	A4	4-6-2	LNER Doncaster 1870	1938	Gresley	LNER
4771	60800	98771	Green Arrow	V2	2-6-2	LNER Doncaster 1837	1936	Gresley	LNER
3442	61994	98642	The Great Marquess	K4	2-6-0	LNER Darlington 1761	1938	Gresley	LNER
1306	61306	—	Mayflower*	B1	4-6-0	North British 26207	1948	Thompson	BR
2005	62005	98605		K1	2-6-0	North British 26609	1949	Peppercorn	BR
75069	75069	98469		4	4-6-0	BR Swindon	1955	Riddles	BR
80079	80079	98479		4MT	2-6-4T	BR Brighton	1954	Riddles	BR
80080	80080	98480		4MT	2-6-4T	BR Brighton	1954	Riddles	BR
92203	92203	—	Black Prince*	9F	2-10-0	BR Swindon	1959	Riddles	BR
92220	92220	98920	Evening Star	9F	2-10-0	BR Swindon	1960	Riddles	BR

* Names given since acquisition for preservation.

GWR Types
No. 3440/3717 *City of Truro*

William Dean was Locomotive, Carriage & Wagon Superintendent (forerunner of the position of Chief Mechanical Engineer) of the Great Western Railway until he was succeeded in May 1902 by George Jackson Churchward. Dean was responsible for the beautiful double-framed designs of the Victorian age, but from 1897 when Churchward had been appointed as chief assistant to Dean, it was Churchward's influence which slowly came to the fore. In April 1900 the 'Atbara' class 4-4-0 was introduced, which in a sense, was a compromise of Dean and Churchward designs.

Forty 'Atbara' 4-4-0s had been built by late 1901, and it was one of these, No. 3405 *Mauritious* which was rebuilt in September 1902 and became the first of the famous 'City' class 4-4-0s. Ten new 'City' locomotives were delivered during 1903 including No. 3440 *City of Truro* which appeared in May, while a further nine 'Atbaras' were rebuilt between 1907 and 1909, making a total class of twenty. These locomotives represented the peak of Churchward's development of the Dean inside-cylinder double-frame 4-4-0 but they were soon replaced by Churchward's outside-cylinder 4-6-0 designs on the principal express trains. However, No. 3440 *City of Truro* made history in May 1904 with a claimed top speed of 102.3mph descending from Whiteball Summit whilst working a five-vehicle mail train from Plymouth to London.

The first of the 'Citys' was withdrawn in 1927 and scrapping of all twenty was looking a distinct possibility by 1930 when only three, including *City of Truro* were still in service. It was Collett who suggested to the LNER that *City of Truro* might be preserved and given a home in the then new railway museum at York. Happily it was preserved (in later superheated form) and arrived at York in 1931 having been withdrawn in March of that year. It remained there until January 1957 when it was extricated from the museum and restored to working order for the first time for hauling special trains. It was also used on a number of ordinary service trains, but was retired again in 1961 and despatched to the GWR Railway Museum at Swindon.

In July 1984 it was again taken off museum display and transported by road to the Severn Valley Railway where it was once again restored to working order for the GW150 celebrations in 1985. Finished in 1903-style livery it has worked on the Severn Valley Railway and on the main line, and has now been transferred to the National Railway Museum at York from where it makes periodic main line outings.

Following overhaul No. 3440 *City of Truro* made a return to main line running on 20th October 1985 with a train from Gloucester to Newport and return formed of InterCity painted stock. It is seen on the outward run accelerating away from a stop at Lydney.

John Whiteley

During the summer of 1986 *City of Truro* was used on "Scarborough Spa Expresses", and on 6th August it is seen on the outward journey shortly after passing Malton.

Gavin Morrison

City of Truro has double-headed on the main line on a number of occasions, and with a sprinkling of snow on the ground, it is seen coupled ahead of No. 4930 *Hagley Hall* on 30th December 1985 passing Droitwich Spa. They are hauling an excursion which originated from King's Cross, including a steam section between Kidderminster and Hereford.

John Whiteley

Seen near Haxby on 20th December 1986, No. 3440 is again heading for Scarborough hauling the "Dickens Festival Express".

Gavin Morrison

Later on the crisp winter's day of 20th December 1986, No. 3440 is negotiating the curves near Kirkham Priory with the River Derwent in the background, whilst returning to York.

John Whiteley

No. 2857

Churchward was responsible for introducing the first 2-8-0 tender engine to this country when the prototype No. 97 (later renumbered 2800) appeared in June 1903. It was the first of 167 2800 class two-cylinder 2-8-0 heavy freight engines, which were initially intended for heavy coal traffic. No. 2857 appeared in May 1918 and was in the last batch of 28 engines which were completed during 1918 and 1919, bringing the class total at that time to 84. So successful was the design that Collett started building them again in 1938 with only a few alterations and a further 83 engines were built between 1938 and 1942, Nos 2884-2899 and 3800-3866.

They were all built at Swindon, and although the early engines were built without outside steampipes, from 1934 onwards outside steampipes were fitted to most of the class. Their high tractive effort and small coupled wheels of 4ft 7^1/2in made them ideal for the use for which they were designed, but eventually they found their way onto most types of freight working throughout the GWR system, and even were pressed into passenger use occasionally. In the 1948 Locomotive Exchanges one of the later 2884 series, No. 3803, was used in the trials to assist with the preparation of designs for new BR standard steam locomotives, tribute indeed to a design which was then almost 50 years old!

No. 2857 was withdrawn in April 1963 and rescued from Woodham's Barry scrapyard by the 2857 Fund in August 1975 and restored to working order on the Severn Valley Railway in green livery, as was initially given to these engines before the First World War.

As part of the GW150 celebrations in 1985 an exhibition of freight traffic was staged at Newport on 10th September, including old and new motive power. No. 2857 was the steam participant and it is seen here leaving Alexandra Dock Junction, Newport, with a mock freight bound for Kidderminster.

J.R.P. Hunt

A run past was organised at Newport station, shortly after which No. 2857 is seen accelerating away towards Eask Usk Junction on the 'up' slow line, with an HST just visible in the background on the 'down' fast line.

J.R.P. Hunt

No. 4555

In 1904 Churchward introduced a small class of 2-6-2T light tank engine for branch line work. It had two outside cylinders and 4ft 1$\frac{1}{2}$in coupled wheels and was known as the 4400 class. Although very successful and capable of remarkable acceleration, Churchward felt that an increase in coupled wheel diameter would produce a more generally useful engine capable of a higher speed, and with this in mind he introduced the 4500 class 2-6-2T light tank engine.

Although the general dimensions remained the same, the 4500 class had 4ft 7$\frac{1}{2}$in coupled wheels, and the first batch of twenty was built at Wolverhampton between 1906 and 1908. These were the last new locomotives to be built there, future construction being concentrated at Swindon. Subsequent batches were built at Swindon between 1909 and 1924 until 75 were in service. A further 100 were built between 1927 and 1929 but these were to a slightly different design, including larger water tanks and this series was referred to as the 4575 class.

No. 4555 was completed in 1924 and had outside steampipes, enlarged bunker and improved superheat-ing, unlike the earlier engines, many of which were modified later. These delightful little engines were to be seen on branch line work throughout the West Country and elsewhere on lines of the GWR, and all survived Nationalisation. BR initially painted these engines black, but in their latter years they received fully lined-out BR green which suited them exceedingly well. The first of the class to be withdrawn was No. 4531 in 1950, but several of these "Small Prairie" tanks of Classes 4500 and 4575 have survived, including No. 4555 which was purchased by Mr. Patrick Whitehouse and Mr. P. J. Garland at a price which included a heavy intermediate repair at Swindon, a test run and a spare boiler. It was repainted at Tyseley in full GWR livery, and whilst at Tyseley worked a number of special and also some local passenger and freight services on the Snow Hill to Leamington line, no doubt to the surprise of local commuters! In 1966 it moved to Totnes for use on the Dart Valley Railway, since when it has worked regularly on both the Dart Valley and Torbay sections.

On 2nd May 1964 No. 4555 and Collett 0-6-0PT No. 3690 worked the Stephenson Locomotive Society last train to Brecon special, and the pair are seen arriving at Pontsticill Junction on the return from Brecon to Cardiff.

J.D. Mills

Also on 2nd May 1964, Nos 4555 and 3690 are seen leaving Brecon with the last train to Merthyr over the ex-Brecon & Merthyr Railway on the return to Cardiff.

J.D. Mills

On 19th September 1965 No. 4555 was paired with No. 1420 (see page 33) to haul a Stephenson Locomotive Society special to Bewdley, and the pair are seen near Worcester.

Ivo Peters

Another picture taken on 19th September 1965 shows Nos 4555 and 1420 emerging from Rainbow Hill Tunnel, Worcester, on the way to Bewdley.

A.A. Vickers

No. 4079 *Pendennis Castle*

C. B. Collett succeeded Churchward as Chief Mechanical Engineer of the Great Western Railway on 1st January 1922 at a difficult time, when Britain's railways were being formed into four main groups. However, unlike the other three new companies which came into being on 1st January 1923 – the LMS, LNER and Southern, the Great Western retained its original identity – it simply became enlarged. Its locomotive affairs remained centred at Swindon and its standard express passenger engine at the time was the four-cylinder 'Star' class which had been built by Churchward in several different batches from 1906.

The 'Stars' were exceptional engines and formed the basis of the design for the more powerful engine which Collett produced in 1923 – the 4073 class 4-6-0 four-cylinder express passenger engine – the 'Castle' class. Although a new boiler was designed for the 'Castles' and the diameter of the cylinders increased, the layout of the frames and the spacing of the 6ft 8½in coupled wheels was the same as the 'Stars'. The Civil Engineer's 20 ton axle load restriction was not exceeded but the new 'Castles' were at least 10% more powerful than the 'Stars' and succeeded them as the standard GWR express passenger locomotive.

No. 4073 *Caerphilly Castle* was completed at Swindon in August 1923 and a further nine engines of this first batch of ten, Nos 4073–4082 were all completed at Swindon between December 1923 and April 1924. No. 4079 *Pendennis Castle* appeared in February 1924 and soon took up 'Star' turns on GWR expresses. It will always be remembered, however, for its part in the GWR-LNER locomotive exchange of 1925 when it was tested against the performance of the Gresley LNER Class A1 Pacifics between King's Cross and Doncaster. During the actual trials on the week of 27th April to 2nd May 1925 *Pendennis Castle* regularly lifted its 475 ton trains past Finsbury Park in under six minutes and arrived early at Peterborough and Doncaster with very economical fuel consumption. Similar results were obtained by No. 4074 *Caldicot Castle* competing against No. 4474 *Victor Wild* on the "Cornish Riviera" between Paddington and Plymouth. Not surprisingly LNER officials were staggered and Gresley was quick to learn from the results of the Churchward/Collett longer travel valve gear and higher steam pressure. The 'Castles' were built over a period of no less than 28 years with only minor changes to the original specification, and eventually totalled 171 engines. A few were rebuilt from 'Stars' and one nominally from Churchward's Pacific No. 111 *The Great Bear*. *Pendennis Castle* was withdrawn in May 1964 and acquired for preservation, but after working a series of specials on the main line, was sold in 1977 to Hamersley Iron Company and shipped to Australia.

After being bought for preservation, No. 4079 *Pendennis Castle* became the last steam locomotive to be overhauled at Swindon Works in the steam era. Its first run on the main line after restoration was in August 1965, but it is seen here, pausing for a photographic stop at Ashchurch on 20th November 1965 with a Locomotive Club of Great Britain special to the Midlands.

Gavin Morrison

To mark the end of through passenger services from Paddington to Birkenhead, two specials were run on 4th March 1967, steam hauled between Didcot and Chester by No. 7029 *Clun Castle* and No. 4079 *Pendennis Castle* respectively. In this picture *Pendennis Castle* is approaching Ruabon on the outward journey.
Gavin Morrison

Following purchase by its new Australian owners, *Pendennis Castle* worked a farewell main line tour from Saltley to Didcot on 29th May 1977, and is seen here on the return journey approaching Culham, shortly after leaving Didcot.

John Whiteley

On the outward journey of the "Great Western Envoy" of Sunday 29th May 1977, *Pendennis Castle* is standing at Aynho Junction signal box, before setting back and working wrong line due to engineering work further south.

John Whiteley

No. 5051 *Drysllwyn Castle/Earl Bathurst*

No. 5051 was built at Swindon in May 1936 and initially was named *Drysllwyn Castle,* but was renamed *Earl Bathurst* in August 1937. The locomotive is preserved, however, in its original condition but has the slightly shorter single chimney which was introduced as standard for the 'Castles' soon after No. 5051 was built. The locomotive cost £4,848 to build in 1936 and was allocated to Landore shed, Swansea where it stayed until April 1961. It had a brief spell at Neath before being moved to Llanelly in February 1963 from where it was withdrawn in May 1963, having covered just over 1,300,000 miles in revenue–earning service. Fortunately it found the haven of Woodham Bros scrapyard at Barry in South Wales and languished there for almost seven years before being bought by the Great Western Society. It was transferred to Didcot in February 1970 and restoration as No. 5051 *Drysllwyn Castle* took almost ten years to complete. It has also carried its *Earl Bathurst* name on occasions since restoration.

No. 5051 *Drysllwyn Castle* appeared on the main line just in time to haul the Great Western Society chocolate and cream liveried Vintage train. It is seen here in unlined austerity World War II livery climbing out of Stratford upon Avon towards Wilmcote on 26th January 1980 with "The Sunset" railtour which was the last main line outing of the GWS Vintage train.

John Whiteley

A much published scene, but nevertheless a magnificent spectacle as *Dryslwyn Castle* and *Hagley Hall* emerge into the sunshine at Horse Cove, near Dawlish, on 7th July 1985 hauling the "Great Western Limited" GW150 special to Plymouth, which was steam hauled from Bristol.

John Whiteley

On 9th October 1982 *Drysllwyn Castle* worked the "Devonian", a special from Didcot to Birmingham Moor Street, via Stratford upon Avon, and is seen here near Danzey on the North Warwicks line on the outward journey.

John Whiteley

On 17th March 1984 No. 5051 needs every ounce of power to lift a heavy twelve-coach northbound "Welsh Marches Express" up the gradient towards Pontypool Road, seen near Cwmbran.

John Whiteley

On the evening of 7th September 1985 *Drysll-wyn Castle* stands on shed at Laira prior to working a Plymouth-Bristol train the following day with *Clun Castle*.

John Whiteley

Another view of *Drysllwyn Castle* at Laira after the open day, as part of the GW150 celebrations. Above the cabside number can be seen the power group and route classification applied to the 'Castles': D, Red. The fully lined out GWR livery can also be seen to advantage.

John Whiteley

No. 5080 *Defiant*

A fourth 'Castle' class 4-6-0 has now been restored and seen duty on the main line, in the shape of No. 5080 *Defiant*. It was completed at Swindon Works in May 1939 and until January 1941 was named *Ogmore Castle*. Initially it worked from Old Oak Common, but in the summer of 1940 it was transferred to Cardiff Canton where it was renamed *Defiant* to commemorate a famous type of aircraft which had been involved in the Battle of Britain. Whilst allocated to Cardiff Canton it participated in the main diagrams and was a regular performer on Paddington services from South Wales. In 1956 it was transferred to Carmarthen and subsequently had spells at Landore, Carmarthen and Llanelly, from where it was withdrawn in April 1963. Initially the 'Britannia' Standard Pacifics had ousted the South Wales 'Castles' from the principal London workings, but in turn the 'Britannias' were replaced after the arrival of BR's main line diesel hydraulic locomotives.

Unlike some of the 'Castles', *Defiant* was never fitted with a double chimney and on withdrawal went to Barry for scrap. In 1973 it was purchased by the Standard Gauge Steam Trust at Tyseley, initially for spare parts for No. 7029 *Clun Castle*. However, full restoration was eventually completed at the now named Birmingham Railway Museum and its planned main line debut was scheduled for 5th September 1987 between Swansea and Carmarthen. Sadly this was cancelled because of mechanical problems and it finally appeared on 11th June 1988, once again proudly displaying "The Red Dragon" headboard.

On 11th June 1988 the inaugural main line run of No. 5080 *Defiant* took it from Dorridge to Didcot. On the return it is seen climbing the lower reaches of Hatton Bank with its twelve coach train.

Pete Skelton

No. 7029 *Clun Castle*

No. 7029 *Clun Castle* was in the final batch of ten 'Castles' which were built at Swindon in 1950 under BR auspices, and thus never carried Great Western livery in ordinary service. Very few modifications had been made over the years to the 'Castles', a fine tribute to the original design, but the post-war engines, with F. W. Hawksworth now as Chief Mechanical Engineer, were fitted with three-row superheaters and mechanical lubrication for cylinders, valves and regulator.

Following the successful fitting of double blastpipe and chimneys to the 'Kings' from 1955, No. 7018 *Dryslwyn Castle* (not to be confused with No. 5051 which is now preserved) was fitted with a double blastpipe and chimney in 1956, but retaining its three-row superheater. In April 1957 No. 4090 *Dorchester Castle* was the second 'Castle' to be rebuilt with a double chimney, but with a four-row superheater, and this set the pattern for the final improvement to the class. A total of 66 'Castles' were rebuilt in this manner

in their final years including *Clun Castle* which was rebuilt in October 1959 and in which form it can be seen today.

These rebuilt 'Castles' were producing some sparkling performances, often being timed at speeds around 100mph, until they were displaced by the main line diesel hydraulics, and in May 1964 *Clun Castle* was timed at 96mph when working part of a high speed special between Plymouth and Bristol. It had the distinction of working the last official BR steam train out of Paddington on 11th June 1965.

In common with other post-war 'Castles' of the 7000 series, *Clun Castle* had years of useful life left when it was withdrawn in December 1965. Fortunately Mr Patrick Whitehouse secured its purchase and it ultimately passed to 7029 Clun Castle Ltd at Tyseley and can now be seen both on the main line and at its home at the Birmingham Railway Museum.

'Castles' were no strangers to fierce gradients, notably the South Devon Banks and the Cornish main line. However, following preservation No. 7029 *Clun Castle* tackled the northern fells and on 14th October 1967 is approaching Shap Summit.

Gavin Morrison

Again, far from the usual haunts of a 'Castle', No. 7029 is nearing the summit of the "long drag" at Blea Moor, on the Settle and Carlisle line, with a special from York to Carlisle on 30th September 1967.

John Whiteley

On 9th September 1967 *Clun Castle* worked a special on the East Coast Main Line and is seen leaving York for Newcastle.

John Whiteley

Clun Castle is approaching Gobowen Junction on 4th March 1967 with "The Zulu" special to Birkenhead. (see also page 15).

Gavin Morrison

On Sunday 8th September 1985 impressive motive power for the return "Great Western Limited" from Plymouth to Bristol was provided in the shape of *Clun Castle* and *Drysllwyn Castle*. The pair of 'Castles' are seen accelerating the train away from Exeter St Davids towards Cowley Bridge Junction.   *John Whiteley*

As part of the GW150 celebrations *Clun Castle* worked a special from Plymouth to Truro on Friday 6th September 1985. It is seen coming off the Royal Albert Bridge on the return train from Truro.   *John Whiteley*

No. 4930 *Hagley Hall*

When Collett succeeded Churchward as CME of the GWR there was a need for a mixed-traffic engine, and rather than rebuild Churchward's 4300 Class 2-6-0 he decided to modify a 'Saint' class two-cylinder 4-6-0. In 1924 he rebuilt No. 2925 *Saint Martin* which had been delivered in 1907, the major modifications being the reduction from 6ft 8½in to 6ft coupled wheels and new side window cab. For almost three years this prototype was tested, but then 80 engines were ordered from Swindon which were virtually the same as the prototype but for the provision of outside steam pipes and other detail alterations. No. 2925 was renumbered 4900 in December 1928 while No. 4930 *Hagley Hall* of this first batch was built in May 1929 and attached to a Collett 3,500 gallon tender which was later replaced by the larger 4,000 gallon type.

Several further batches of 'Halls' were built until the last one was delivered in April 1943 when the class totalled 259. Construction of the 'Modified Halls' commenced in 1944 with Hawksworth as CME.

The 'Halls' were truly a mixed-traffic engine and were at home on all types of train throughout the whole of the GWR system, but rarely strayed away from their home lines due to loading gauge restrictions. *Hagley Hall* spent a lot of time in the West Country, but in later years it was allocated to Old Oak Common and Swindon. It was withdrawn in December 1963 having covered just over 1¼ million miles in its 34 years of service. Fortuitously it was sold to Woodham Brothers for scrap and languished in their yard at Barry for eight years before being rescued by the Severn Valley Railway and moved to Bewdley in 1973. Renovation was completed by Bridgnorth and if it was not for the efforts of the amateur railway preservationists not one of the GWR's two-cylinder mixed-traffic engines would have survived, none being part of the National Collection! *Hagley Hall*, as well as being seen on the main line, is a regular performer on the Severn Valley Railway.

The late afternoon sun of 22nd September 1979 at Rednall reflects beautifully from the "Inter-City" special returning from Chester to Hereford. Motive power is provided by No. 4930 *Hagley Hall* and Stanier 'Black Five' No. 5000. This was *Hagley Hall's* inaugural main line trip following restoration and initially it was coupled to a Hawksworth straight sided tender from a 'Castle'.

John Whiteley

Hagley Hall, paired with a new tender and No. 7819 *Hinton Manor* are seen on 8th April 1985 accelerating away from Taunton towards Cogload Junction with the "Great Western Limited", returning from Plymouth to Bristol. *Hagley Hall* had been hastily despatched to Plymouth by the Severn Valley Railway the previous day following the failure of *King George V* on the outward train.

John Whiteley

On the dismal morning of 17th October 1981 *Hagley Hall* passes an attractive GWR lower quadrant signal at Sutton Bridge Junction, Shrewsbury, with a southbound "Welsh Marches Pullman".

John Whiteley

Hagley Hall is passing Ponthir on 14th March 1981 and has just started the long climb to Pontypool Road with the "Welsh Marches Express" returning from Newport to Hereford.

John Whiteley

No. 5900 *Hinderton Hall*

Following the first batch of 80 'Halls' which were built after the prototype had been thoroughly tested, No. 5900 *Hinderton Hall* was the last of the second batch of 20 engines which were ordered with only minor detail changes, and it appeared from Swindon in March 1931.

Whilst the 'Halls' were introduced as mixed-traffic engines and throughout their careers handled express passenger traffic over the whole of the GWR system, it is fair to say that they were at their best on heavy fitted freights benefiting from their sure-footedness and excellent free steaming taper boilers. No doubt the experience William Stanier gained from working as Collett's principal assistant on the GWR helped greatly with his design of the "Black Five" for the LMS, which in many respects was similar to the design of the 'Halls'.

On introduction the 'Halls' were given standard GWR green livery but after Nationalisation were painted in the BR mixed-traffic lined black, reverting to lined Brunswick green livery from Summer 1955. The prototype 'Hall', No. 4900 *Saint Martin* was the first of the class to be withdrawn, in 1959, excepting No. 4911 *Bowden Hall* which was withdrawn in 1941 after suffering bomb damage. No. 5900 *Hinderton Hall* was withdrawn in December 1963 and was one of many GWR engines which ended up in the Barry scrapyard. It was purchased by the Great Western Society and painstakingly restored to main line running order, and is now based at the Society's headquarters at Didcot.

Hinderton Hall's main line debut was on 15th May 1976 when it double-headed with No. 6998 *Burton Agnes Hall* on the GWS vintage train. The pair are climbing Hatton Bank en route from Didcot to Dorridge.
L.A. Nixon

No. 5900 *Hinderton Hall* has appeared only rarely on the main line since restoration, one of those occasions being on 3rd March 1979 when it worked the "Shakespeare Venturer" in place of *King George V* which had failed. It is seen here approaching Upper Heyford station.
Pete Skelton

No. 6000 *King George V*

Following his earlier 'Castles' for the GWR, Collett's magnificent four-cylinder 'King' class 4-6-0 first appeared in 1927 from Swindon in the shape of No. 6000 *King George V*. As train loads steadily increased the 'Castles' were not considered powerful enough and in the mid-1920s parts of the GWR main line were increased from 20 ton to 22¹/₂ ton axle loading to accommodate the 'Kings'. As their sphere of operation was to be much more limited than the 'Castles', only a relatively small number were required, and in the event 30 were built between 1927 and 1930 for use between Paddington and Plymouth via Bristol or Westbury and Paddington and Wolverhampton. With their heavy axle loading and 6ft 6in diameter coupled wheels they were very sure-footed engines capable of hauling heavy loads and performed extremely well over the South Devon banks between Newton Abbot and Plymouth, but there even they had to be piloted on the heavier trains. Very few changes were made to the 'Kings' during the reign of Collett as CME of the GWR until he retired in 1941 and was replaced by F. W. Hawksworth. In the post-war days Hawksworth experimented with increased superheating in an attempt to improve performance with inferior coal supplies, and although this proved to be a success with No. 6022 *King Edward III* the modifications were not implemented with the rest of the class until the early 1950s, when four-row superheaters were fitted together with improved draughting for the single chimneys. Following the improved draughting a double chimney was fitted to No. 6015 *King Richard III* in September 1955, and subsequently the entire class was fitted with double chimneys and self-cleaning smokeboxes, No. 6000 being dealt with in December 1956. This succeeded in rejuvenating them and it is in this condition that No. 6000 is now preserved.

Throughout their career the 'Kings' did not stray far from their original routes or allocations of Old Oak Common, Plymouth Laira and Wolverhampton Stafford Road, although at times they were allocated to Newton Abbot, Bristol and latterly Cardiff Canton. They did not suffer the indignity of being relegated to secondary duties, the entire class being withdrawn during 1962, although No. 6018 *King Henry VI* was taken out of store in April 1963 to work an enthusiasts' special. *King George V* was withdrawn in December 1962 having covered almost two million miles and was preserved as part of the National Collection. Its intended destination was the Great Western Museum at Swindon but in 1968 H. P. Bulmers of Hereford commenced complete restoration of the locomotive and eventually secured its return to main line running in 1971, following lengthy negotiations with BR.

Attractively framed, on 18th February 1984 No. 6000 *King George V* approaches Church Stretton with a southbound "Welsh Marches Express", and is almost at the end of the long climb out of Shrewsbury.

Gavin Morrison

A panned picture of *King George V* taken near Pandy as it worked from Hereford to Newport on a "Welsh Marches Pullman" on 10th October 1981, shows the beautifully proportioned design of a 'King' in full flight. The early BR lion and wheel emblem can be seen on the tender, one of the cab roof ventilators which were introduced from 1954, and the special double red route classification below the cab numberplate which was applicable only to the 'Kings'.

John Whiteley

On 18th February 1984 No. 6000 is emerging from Ludlow Tunnel with a southbound "Welsh Marches Express". The bell above the bufferbeam was presented to commemorate the part *King George V* played in the Baltimore & Ohio Railroad centenary celebrations in 1927, and it was also given two small commemorative medals for each of the cabsides which can be seen above the cabside numberplate.

Gavin Morrison

King George V's famous main line run on 2nd October 1971 heralded the start of it all, and who could have optimistically forecast nearly 20 years ago that BR's initial limited approval of a return to main line steam running would lead to such a wealth of lovingly restored locomotives emerging once again. At the head of the train of Bulmer's privately preserved Pullman coaches, *King George V* is seen climbing towards Pilning from the Severn Tunnel on the Newport-Didcot-Oxford section of the day's outing from Hereford to Tyseley on 2nd October 1971.
John Whiteley

With a rather uncharacteristic dark exhaust No. 6000 is accelerating hard away from Standish Junction on 12th October 1985 with the "Red Dragon" special from Swindon to Gloucester, Newport and Hereford.
John Whiteley

No. 6106

A succession of 2-6-2T passenger tank engines were introduced by Churchward and the initial 3100 class of 1903 was eventually multiplied to 306 engines in six sub-divisions, some of which were not completed until after Nationalisation. The 6100 series were basically similar to the earlier 5101 class of 1929 but had an increased boiler pressure. A total of 70 were built at Swindon in three separate batches between 1931 and 1935, No. 6106 appearing in May 1931.

These fine Prairie Tanks of the 6100 series were built specifically to improve the London surburban services of the early 1930s and were only to be seen with any regularity elsewhere after the mid-1950s, their demise eventually brought about by the introduction of diesel multiple units. The first of the class to be withdrawn was No. 6100 in 1958, but the last nine survived until 1965, by this time working on a variety of lesser duties. Prior to withdrawal No. 6106 spent some time at Gloucester and was used on banking duties to Sapperton from the sub-shed at Brimscombe on the "Golden Valley" route.

After withdrawal No. 6106 was purchased privately and can now be seen at the Great Western Society headquarters at Didcot Railway Centre, which is a somewhat ironic twist of fate because in 1962 this locomotive was in store at Didcot and may well have been withdrawn for scrapping. As luck would have it, instead it was given a heavy overhaul at Swindon and returned to traffic, working from Southall. After No. 6106 had been withdrawn from BR service and secured for the Great Western Society it was the first of their preserved locomotives to arrive at Didcot when they transferred their headquarters to there in November 1967.

Saturday 4th November 1967 was a memorable day in the history of the Great Western Society, being the day their headquarters were transferred to Didcot from Taplow to open a new phase in the preservation movement. No. 6106 is seen nearing Didcot on that day, in the process of rounding up miscellaneous stock for Didcot. It had travelled from Taplow to Kensington Olympia to pick up two Pullman cars, returned to Taplow to collect two "Ocean Saloons", Nos 9112 and 9118 (2nd and 3rd vehicles) and also a BR utility van full of spare parts.

Patrick Russell

No. 6435

The 6400 class 0-6-0 pannier tank light passenger tank engine was introduced by Collett in 1932 as a development of his earlier 5400 class 0-6-0PT of 1931. The 6400 class was built with smaller coupled wheels of 4ft 7^1/$_2$in which made them more suitable for use on the more steeply graded routes, such as South Wales where the majority of the class were initially allocated.

A total of 40 6400 class 0-6-0PTs were built in four batches at Swindon between 1932 and 1937, No. 6435 being in the last batch of ten built in 1937. All 40 were fitted for auto-train working, and apart from South Wales a few could be seen at Laira and in the West

Midlands. The 6400 class pannier tank altered little in appearance through the years, but eventually they were fitted with a top feed on the boiler and a large whistle shield in front of the cab. The first of these useful engines was withdrawn in 1958, but as dieselisation progressed and branch line closure accelerated the duties for which they were originally intended had all but disappeared by the mid-1960s. Fortunately three have been preserved and No. 6435 can now be seen on the Dart Valley Railway in Devon, having been purchased privately.

On Sunday 17th October 1965 a Stephenson Locomotive Society special ran between Birmingham Snow Hill and Bristol. Between Birmingham and Gloucester the train was hauled by Nos 1420 (see page 33) and 6435. On the Gloucester avoiding line No. 1420 was replaced by *Clun Castle*, still in BR service, and the pair are seen near Gloucester South Junction.

Gavin Morrison

No. 6435 worked another Stephenson Locomotive Society special, on 24th April 1965, and is seen between Stratford upon Avon and Stratford Old Town on its way to Woodford Halse on the now long gone ex-Stratford upon Avon & Midland Junction Railway.

T.E. Williams

32

No. 1420

In 1932 Collett introduced his delightful 4800 class 0-4-2T primarily for light auto-train working and a total of 75 were built between 1932 and 1936, all of which had auto-train gear and ATC apparatus. A separate 5800 class of 20 engines was built in 1933, but these were introduced without either auto-train or ATC apparatus. All the 4800 class were renumbered 1400-1474 in 1946 when some of their original numbers in the 4800 series were required by 20 2800 class 2-8-0s which had been equipped for oil burning. The 0-4-2Ts were then redesignated the 1400 class.

No. 1420 was built in 1932 and although these 0-4-2Ts were sprightly performers, their axle-loading was less than 14 tons and their total weight was only just in excess of 41 tons which allowed them to work throughout the GWR system on their network of rural branch lines. Withdrawal commenced in 1956 due to the closure of the branch lines they worked and the introduction of diesel railcars, but a few, including No. 1420 soldiered on until 1964. No. 1420 was finally withdrawn in November 1964, and subsequently purchased and preserved on the Dart Valley Railway in Devon, where it is now named *Bulliver*.

The first of two more pictures taken on 17th October 1965 of the SLS "Great Western Cavalcade" railtour from Birmingham Snow Hill to Bristol, used to transfer Nos 1420 and 6435 to the Dart Valley Railway. The pair are seen about to depart from Worcester Shrub Hill.

Gavin Morrison

A stop at Ashchurch gives participants and others an opportunity to have a close look at the two locomotives. No. 1420 travelled light engine to Bristol after it was replaced at Gloucester by *Clun Castle*, and from Bristol Nos 1420 and 6435 proceeded to the Dart Valley Railway, the SLS special returning to Birmingham behind *Clun Castle*.

Gavin Morrison

No. 1466

No. 1466 was built at Swindon in 1936 as No. 4866 in the last batch of 15 of these classical Collett GWR branch line engines. They were originally turned out in pre-war GWR plain green livery, but subsequently were given BR plain black livery which in turn was replaced by plain green from 1956. Several received BR fully lined-out green livery from 1957. The auto-fitted 1400 class will always be associated with the delights of a GWR rural branch line and one of them was featured in the famous comedy film "The Titfield Thunderbolt".

These 0-4-2Ts were far from life-expired when withdrawn from BR service and it is not surprising that four examples have been preserved. The Great Western Society started a 14xx preservation fund in the early days of the Society's existence and in February 1964 acquired No. 1466 from BR for £750. It had been withdrawn from Taunton shed and was transferred to Totnes, the first base of the Great Western Society. On 2nd December 1967 it was coupled inside No. 6998 *Burton Agnes Hall* for the journey from Devon to Didcot, the new home of the Great Western Society where it can still be seen.

The Wallingford branch from the main line at Cholsey & Moulsford closed to passengers in June 1959, but on 15th April 1968 the Great Western Society operated the branch with an auto-train consisting of No. 1466 and auto trailer No. W231W which was built by BR in 1951 to a GWR design. It is seen here being propelled towards Wallingford.

W.M.J. Jackson

The train terminated at the Associated British Maltsters' factory, a few hundred yards from the site of Wallingford station, and No. 1466 is seen restarting a train to Cholsey & Moulsford.

W.M.J. Jackson

No. 7808 *Cookham Manor*

By 1938 a considerable number of 'Hall' class 4-6-0s were already in service and the 'Grange' 4-6-0s had also been introduced as a logical mixed-traffic development from the 'Halls' – sadly a 'Grange' has not survived.

However, there was still a need for a light mixed-traffic engine to allow withdrawal of various ageing 2-6-0 and 4-4-0 designs and to implement this scheme Collett designed the two-cylinder 'Manor' class 4-6-0. It was his final 4-6-0 design for the GWR and the first ten, including No. 7808 *Cookham Manor*, were all built at Swindon in 1938. A total of 30 'Manors' were built at Swindon and the first 20 all utilised the wheels and motion of withdrawn Churchward 4300 class 2-6-0s.

As introduced the 'Manors' were disappointing performers and were noted for their rather poor steaming characteristics. In an attempt to improve matters tests were carried out in the early 1950s with No. 7818 *Granville Manor*, after which draughting improvements were implemented to the whole class and a redesigned chimney fitted. After these steaming problems had been cured the 'Manors' became very popular engines with footplatemen and with their light axle-loading of just over 17 tons were suitable for use almost anywhere on the GWR system.

No. 7808 *Cookham Manor* covered almost one million miles in BR service before being withdrawn from Gloucester in December 1965. It was purchased by a Great Western Society member and moved to the Dowty Railway Preservation Society base at Ashchurch. It was restored to main line running condition and now operates from its base at Didcot.

19th October 1974 was a milestone in the history of the Great Western Society. Following meticulous restoration work, it was the first occasion that a complete GWS vintage train was allowed out on the main line. It comprised seven vehicles including the "Ocean Saloon" No. 9118 *Princess Elizabeth* hauled by No. 7808 *Cookham Manor* and No. 6998 *Burton Agnes Hall*. The train ran from Didcot to Stratford upon Avon and Tyseley and is seen here approaching Wilmcote on the climb from Stratford upon Avon.

John Whiteley

Cookham Manor and *Burton Agnes Hall* are seen in tandem again on 14th June 1975 heading a Great Western Society excursion away from Hereford, having travelled from Didcot via Oxford and Worcester.

John Whiteley

To celebrate the 150th anniversary of the Stockton & Darlington Railway, *Cookham Manor* appeared at the Shildon Cavalcade on Sunday 31st August 1975 with four vintage coaches and Siphon G No. 2796 which was built in 1937 as a ventilated bogie vehicle to carry milk churns. The train is seen leaving Chesterfield on the return from Shildon to Didcot on 1st September 1975.

John Whiteley

Marred only by an unsightly headboard, *Cookham Manor* and *Hinderton Hall* look quite magnificent at the head of the GWS Vintage train on 6th October 1979 as they approach Wolvercote Junction, north of Oxford. A sight reminiscent of the pre-Nationalisation period on the GWR.

John Whiteley

No. 7812 *Erlestoke Manor*

No. 7812 *Erlestoke Manor* was built in January 1939, and in common with the other 'Manors' was soon working on the GWR system, particularly on passenger turns on secondary routes where the heavier 'Halls' and 'Granges' were prohibited. The 'Manors' became well known west of Newton Abbot where they were used for banking and pilot duties on the South Devon banks, and on some of the Cornish branch lines. They became best known, however, for their stirling work on the particularly difficult Cambrian line from Shrewsbury to Aberystwyth. They arrived on the Cambrian in 1943, but the transfer from the Western to the London Midland Region in 1963 brought about the gradual elimination of former GWR motive power from the Cambrian.

'Manors' were still to be seen in decreasing numbers on the Cambrian until 1965, their last year of service for BR, and *Erlestoke Manor* was withdrawn in November 1965. It was rescued from Barry scrapyard by the Erlestoke Manor Fund which was formed in the early 1970s, and it was eventually transferred to the Severn Valley Railway in 1976 for restoration. After partial retubing of the boiler *Erlestoke Manor's* return to steam occurred in the summer of 1979. At the end of the 1980 season it was withdrawn from traffic on the Severn Valley Railway for further repair work to BR standards and made its main line debut double-heading with *Hagley Hall* on 24th April 1982.

Beautifully turned out by the Severn Valley Railway in BR lined green livery, No. 7812 *Erlestoke Manor* is piloting its Severn Valley Railway stablemate *Hagley Hall* near Bayston Hill on the climb out of Shrewsbury with a southbound "Welsh Marches Pullman". The date is 24th April 1982 which marked the return of the 'Manor' to main line working.   *John Whiteley*

No. 7819 *Hinton Manor*

No. 7819 *Hinton Manor* was built in February 1939 and was the last of the second batch of ten which also utilised parts from cannibalised 2-6-0s. The final batch of ten 'Manors' was not built until 1950, after both Collett and Hawksworth had disappeared from the GWR scene, and these were entirely new engines and did not incorporate any parts from previously withdrawn engines.

The 'Manors' are generally acknowledged as being amongst the best looking of the GWR 4-6-0s and suited both black livery and fully lined BR Brunswick green which was used from 1956. They were originally introduced for use on the cross country route between Banbury, Cheltenham and Swansea and were the first 4-6-0s allowed on the former Cambrian line. Some were later transferred to Newton Abbot and Plymouth, and Reading latterly had a small allocation for use on the Southern line to Redhill. They were seldom seen in the London area until the last days of steam and *Hinton Manor* was finally withdrawn in November 1965, subsequently rescued from Barry for restoration at the Severn Valley Railway. Apart from its main line use, recently very appropriately on ex-Cambrian lines, it sees regular operation on the Severn Valley Railway between Bridgnorth and Kidderminster.

Easter Sunday 7th April 1985 witnessed the return of main line steam to the South West as part of the GW150 celebrations, but unfortunately not without its problems. No. 7819 *Hinton Manor* and *King George V* left Bristol Temple Meads in fine style with the thirteen coach "Great Western Limited", but as the weather deteriorated, so too did the performance of the locomotives (see also page 50). At Taunton *King George V* was removed from the train having disgraced itself and can be seen on the right hand side of this picture as *Hinton Manor* leaves in pouring rain, banked by a pair of Class 37 diesels for the climb to Whiteball.

John Whiteley

Summer 1987 witnessed the return of steam to the Cambrian. *Hinton Manor* was a regular performer on these trains and is seen on 31st August 1987 near Aberdovey.

D. Phillips

The previous day *Hinton Manor* is seen at Trefri near Penhelig on the Dovey Estuary working a train from Machynlleth to Barmouth.

J.R.P. Hunt

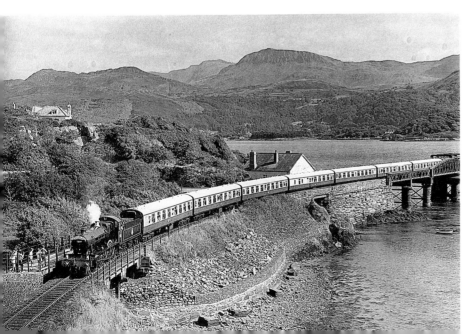

In its attractive early BR lined black livery, *Hinton Manor* is coming off Barmouth Bridge on 30th August 1987. Steam working on this route was made possible as a result of Barmouth Bridge being officially reopened to locomotives on 13th April 1986.

J.R.P. Hunt

Proudly displaying a "Cardigan Bay Express" headboard and an 89C Machynlleth shed plate, *Hinton Manor* takes the Pwllheli line at Dovey Junction with the 09.40 Machynlleth-Barmouth on 25th May 1987.

L.A. Nixon

Having left its Class 37 bankers at Whiteball, *Hinton Manor* speeds past the site of Cullompton station with the "Great Western Limited" on 7th April 1985. However, it had to be removed from the train at Exeter with a hot tender axlebox and the train eventually arrived at Plymouth behind two Class 37 diesel locomotives.

John Whiteley

No. 6960 *Raveningham Hall*

F. W. Hawksworth succeeded C. B. Collett as CME of the GWR in July 1941 during difficult wartime conditions which prevented normal locomotive development. There was, however, a need for mixed-traffic locomotives on the GWR and construction of the 'Hall' class 4-6-0s had continued at Swindon during the war years. Hawksworth recognised the need for a higher degree of superheating in an attempt to combat the effects of poor quality coal and he also simplified the construction of new engines by using main plate frames throughout and a simple plate frame bogie. His 'Modified Hall' two-cylinder 4-6-0 incorporated these new features and the first one, No. 6959 (later *Peatling Hall*) appeared in March 1944.

No. 6960 was one of this first batch of twelve 'Modified Halls' which were all built during 1944 and which appeared in austere black wartime livery without cabside windows or nameplates. All these engines had windows fitted between 1945 and 1948 when they also received nameplates, No. 6960 being named *Raveningham Hall*. These 6959 class 'Modified Halls' were an immediate success with their three-row superheaters, new pattern cylinders and small smokebox saddle which altered their front end appearance slightly from Collett's original 'Halls'. In all a total of 71 'Modified Halls' were built between 1944 and 1950, and the success of the design no doubt paved the way for the BR Standard two-cylinder 4-6-0 designs which followed with R. A. Riddles in charge.

Raveningham Hall had done only 20 years service when it was withdrawn in June 1964, but in common with many other GWR 4-6-0s found the haven of Barry scrapyard. It was spared the cutter's torch when it was acquired and moved to Steamtown, Carnforth where it was restored to main line running condition, subsequently being moved to the Severn Valley Railway.

Complete with "Pembroke Coast Express" headboard, No. 6960 is coasting slowly through Llanelli because of a signal check on its second trip of the day from Carmarthen on 21st September 1985.

Gavin Morrison

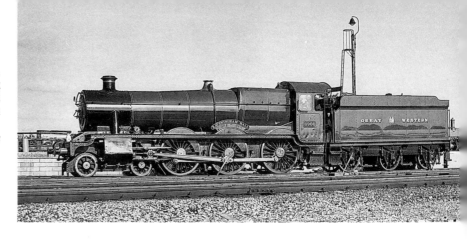

Whilst looking quite magnificent externally, sadly No. 6960 *Raveningham Hall* is standing in the yard at Northallerton on 26th August 1975 having suffered the indignity of a hot box on the way to the Shildon celebrations.

Gavin Morrison

On Sunday 22nd September 1985, another dismal wet day, No. 6960 pulls out of Swansea with a train for Carmarthen as part of the GW150 celebrations.

Gavin Morrison

Seemingly the Severn Valley Railway "bogey" engine, *Raveningham Hall* limps into Chester with a hot box on 8th April 1978 heading the "Cathedrals Express" special. To the disappointment of passengers and onlookers alike a diesel pilot was provided for the return journey.

Gavin Morrison

In September 1985 *Raveningham Hall* worked a series of trains between Swansea and Carmarthen. Now paired with a straight sided tender it is leaving Carmarthen on 22nd September with a train to Swansea.

J.R.P. Hunt

No. 6998 *Burton Agnes Hall*

No. 6998 *Burton Agnes Hall* did not appear until January 1949, one year after Nationalisation, and did a mere 17 years service before being officially withdrawn in December 1965. The 'Modified Halls' had coupled wheels of 6ft diameter, but a wheelbase of 7ft 2in, 2in longer than the original design. Their sphere of operation was also the same as the Collett 'Halls' and a 'Modified Hall', No. 6990 *Witherslack Hall*, was selected as one of three ex-GWR locomotive types for the famous Locomotive Exchange trials of 1948 to assess the capabilities of existing designs, prior to design work on the new BR Standard locomotives. In common with the other Western engines its route availability was somewhat restricted and it ran on Marylebone-Manchester and Bristol-Plymouth trials.

Apart from the first batch of twelve, the remaining 'Modified Halls' were initially fitted with the new pattern straight-sided Hawksworth tender to which *Burton Agnes Hall* is now attached, although tenders were frequently exchanged between locomotives. In early BR days the 'Modified Halls' were given the standard lined black mixed-traffic livery, but from the summer of 1955 were painted in fully lined BR Brunswick green.

As early as August 1965 the Great Western Society had launched a fund to preserve a 'Hall', and in a subsequent ballot had chosen No. 6998 *Burton Agnes Hall* which was due for withdrawal. On 3rd January 1966 it became the last steam locomotive to haul a scheduled passenger train on the Western Region, from Oxford to Banbury and the Great Western Society took delivery of the locomotive at Oxford from where it was moved to Totnes in April 1966, prior to being moved to Didcot on 2nd December 1967. It was restored to main line running condition and hauled the Great Western Society's inaugural train on the main line on 1st October 1972 from Didcot to Tyseley.

In 1986 steam returned to part of the former Southern main line to Exeter, now but a shadow of its former glory having been singled for long sections between Salisbury and Exeter. No. 6998 *Burton Agnes Hall* participated in the workings and on 19th October 1986 is seen nearing Buckhorn Weston Tunnel with a Sunday train from Salisbury to Yeovil Junction. Looking at this 1986 picture, it is hard to believe that this was ever a double track main line.
John Whiteley

On 14th June 1975 *Burton Agnes Hall* is reversing the GWS Vintage train out of Hereford after arrival from Worcester. "Ocean Saloon" No. 9112 *Queen Mary* is next to the engine and "Ocean Saloon" No. 9118 *Princess Elizabeth* is next to that.

John Whiteley

No. 6998 is seen leaving Templecombe on 19th October 1986 with one of the Salisbury-Yeovil Junction specials.

John Whiteley

On 1st October 1972, a glorious autumn day, *Burton Agnes Hall* appeared on the main line for the first time since preservation, working the Great Western Society's inaugural train from Didcot to Tyseley. It is seen here approaching Culham, shortly after leaving Didcot.

John Whiteley

On the way to Tyseley on 1st October 1972 a photographic stop was made at Heyford and *Burton Agnes Hall* is seen shortly after restarting the train.

John Whiteley

Southern Classes

No. 488 (30583)

William Adams was Mechanical Engineer of the London & South Western Railway from 1878 until 1895, during which time he designed a variety of very useful locomotives including a number of extremely elegant tank locomotives. However, he will probably be best remembered for his 415 class (later '0415') 4-4-2Ts, a total of 71 of which were built between 1882 and 1885 for the expanding LSWR suburban passenger services.

Although the first one of these 4-4-2Ts was withdrawn as early as 1916 and only two were in service on the SR by 1928, they remained on the exquisite Lyme Regis branch from Axminster until the end of 1961, by which time they were almost 75 years of age. These two were joined in Devon, just before Nationalisation by a third member of the class which became BR No. 30583. This engine is now preserved on the Bluebell Railway as No. 488 in its LSWR colours and has a particularly interesting history. It was sold by the LSWR to the Ministry of Munitions during the First World War, but in 1919 it was re-sold to the East Kent Railway where it worked as No. 5 until 1939 when it was placed in store. In 1946 it was re-purchased by the Southern Railway and taken back into stock as No. 3488 in the "duplicate" list which was reserved for old locomotives of limited life expectation which had been replaced by newer engines bearing the same number, in this case a Urie H15 4-6-0.

No. 3488 was given a complete overhaul and re-entered service on the Lyme Regis branch with its two sister engines, Nos 3125 and 3520. After Nationalisation they were renumbered 30582–30584 and re-painted in BR lined black livery. They were withdrawn at the end of 1961 when they were replaced by Ivatt 2-6-2Ts, Nos 30582 and 30584 being cut up at Eastleigh Works. Fortunately No. 30583 was purchased by the Bluebell Railway where it can still be seen.

On 15th September 1963 No. 488 pilots No. 473 *Birch Grove* with "The Blue Belle" special. The pair are near Ardingly en route from Haywards Heath to Sheffield Park.

Patrick Russell

Below, right: Another picture of "The Blue Belle" special of 15th September 1963 sees *Birch Grove* and No. 488 approaching Haywards Heath before reversal.

W.M.J. Jackson

No. 473 *Birch Grove* (32473)

Robert J. Billinton was appointed Locomotive, Carriage & Wagon Superintendent of the London, Brighton & South Coast Railway in January 1890, following the sudden death of William Stroudley. He perpetuated some of the Stroudley designs, particularly the tank locomotives which were so much a feature of the LBSCR which operated only approximately 450 route miles and preferred the use of tank locomotives on its relatively short main lines.

Following the introduction of his E3 class 0-6-2Ts in 1894, "small radials" as they became known, he produced his E4 class 0-6-2Ts – "large radials" with larger coupled wheels of 5ft. The first of 75 appeared from Brighton in December 1897, and No. 473 *Birch Grove* appeared in June 1898, having cost just over £2,000 to build. They were particularly successful on both goods and passenger duties and were well-liked by the footplate crews and must have looked very fine in their early livery of Stroudley passenger yellow ochre which was used for some of the class, the remainder being painted Stroudley goods green.

No. 473 *Birch Grove* was initially allocated to New Cross in London but also spent time at Brighton before the Grouping. All the E4s were accepted by the Southern Railway as passenger engines and were painted standard Southern green and renumbered from 1931 by the simple addition of 2000 denoting a former LBSCR engine. Despite being painted passenger green the E4s were used for much of the time from the Grouping on local goods, station pilots or shunting duties and by the mid-1930s many ex-LBSCR locomotives had been withdrawn. However, all but one of the E4s entered British Railways stock in 1948 and were painted in the lined-black secondary passenger engine livery with the addition of 30000 to their numbers. *Birch Grove* was renumbered 32473 in April 1951 at Ashford Works and painted lined-black in April 1954, also at Ashford. By the mid-1950s many Locomotives were surplus to the Southern Region's requirements and withdrawal of the E4s commenced, although even as late as the early 1960s they were occasionally seen on secondary passenger workings in the Brighton and Eastbourne areas.

The last E4 was withdrawn in June 1963 but No. 32473 was sold to the Bluebell Railway on 16th October 1962 having run just over 1,200,000 miles in service. It can still be seen at the Bluebell Railway as No. 473 *Birch Grove* in Marsh umber livery, not historically correct but nevertheless very attractive.

No. 120 (30120)

When William Adams retired as Mechanical Engineer of the London & South Western Railway in 1895 he had already established a reasonable stock of modern locomotives, including a number of 4-4-0s. He was succeeded by Dugald Drummond who assumed the title of Chief Mechanical Engineer of the LSWR in 1905 until he was succeeded by Robert Urie in 1912. Some of Drummond's early designs for the LSWR were far from successful, but as facilities improved on long distance passenger trains such as corridor coaches and catering accommodation, so too schedules had to improve. Like other locomotive engineers of the period he was faced with the need to produce more powerful locomotives and his answer appeared early in 1899 in the shape of his T9 class 4-4-0 which had a larger firebox than his earlier designs and more boiler tubes to provide a very free steaming boiler.

The initial batch of 30 was built by Dübs of Glasgow, with a further one late in 1901, but the remaining 35 were built at Nine Elms, including No. 120 which appeared in August 1899. Until the early 1920s the 66 T9s were handling all the premier passenger trains until they started to be replaced by more modern designs, principally the Urie N15 class 4-6-0s. However, from 1922 all the T9s were superheated and rebuilt with an extended smokebox, including No. 120 in May 1927, with the last one being dealt with in 1929. This transformed their performance and the excellent free running characteristics of the T9s soon earned them the nickname of "Greyhounds".

By the late 1920s the T9s were to be seen on passenger turns on all three Sections of the Southern Railway, having been given plain stove-pipe chimneys to enable them to work on the Central and Eastern Sections. All the T9s were in service at Nationalisation, but withdrawal commenced in 1951, and with the exception of No. 30120, the last ones were withdrawn in July 1961. An exception was made in the case of No. 30120 which was overhauled at Eastleigh Works in March 1962 and emerged in LSWR livery as No. 120 for hauling special trains. It was officially withdrawn in July 1963 but nevertheless continued working until the end of 1963 when it went into store at various locations until becoming part of the reserve collection at the NRM York, but not displayed publicly. Subsequently it was loaned to the Mid-Hants Railway and superbly restored by them to working order in BR lined black livery, and later SR olive green, and has seen regular service betwen Alresford, Ropley and Alton.

Coupled ahead of Class U 2-6-0 No. 31790, T9 class 4-4-0 No. 120 is approaching Woodford Halse in 1963 with an excursion from London.
J.R.P. Hunt

A fabulous scene at Brighton MPD on 15th September 1963 on the occasion of the visit of two very distinguished preserved locomotives for "The Blue Belle" specials. In the foreground is "Terrier" AIx 0-6-0T No. 32640, formerly named *Newport* and now itself preserved on the Isle of Wight Steam Railway. Behind it, being serviced are the "Caley Single" (see page 69) and No. 120, already with a full head of steam prior to its return journey to Victoria.

W.M.J. Jackson

No. 3440 *City of Truro* catches the last rays of the setting sun on 20th December 1986 as it nears Haxby on its way from York to Scarborough.

John Whiteley

As part of the GW150 celebrations No. 7029 *Clun Castle* returns to Plymouth with a train from Truro on 6th September 1985. It is crossing Coombe St Stephen Viaduct, with the piers of the original Cornwall Railway structure visible on the left hand side of the picture.

John Whiteley

No. 6000 *King George V* and No. 7819 *Hinton Manor* are approaching Taunton on 7th April 1985 with the "Great Western Limited". Sadly the 'King' was removed from the train at Taunton and the train eventually arrived at Plymouth behind a pair of Class 37 diesel electric locomotives.

John Whiteley

On 4th March 1967 No. 4079 *Pendennis Castle* passes through Chester in fine style before picking up its train and returning to Didcot with the "Birkenhead Flyer".

John Whiteley

No. 6000 *King George V* has been a regular performer on the North and West route and on 4th October 1980 it is seen accelerating away from Ludlow on its way from Hereford to Chester with the "Deeside Venturer".

John Whiteley

On 18th October 1986 steam returned to part of the former LSWR main line from Waterloo to Exeter in the shape of No. 6998 *Burton Agnes Hall* when it worked a series of trains between Salisbury and Yeovil Junction. In pleasant autumn sunshine it has just passed Tisbury on a section of line which was long since singled and now but a shadow of its former glory.

John Whiteley

On its first southbound solo run over the Settle and Carlisle line, No. 777 *Sir Lamiel* has just emerged from Helm Tunnel with a "Cumbrian Mountain Pullman" on 22nd May 1982.

John Whiteley

Another picture on the Settle and Carlisle line sees No. 850 *Lord Nelson* at Baron Wood on 3rd March 1984 heading a southbound "Cumbrian Mountain Express".

John Whiteley

No. 34092 *City of Wells* is leaving Carlisle in fine style on 13th February 1982 with a southbound "Cumbrian Mountain Pullman". *John Whiteley*

The "East Midlander No. 4" was organised by the Railway Correspondence and Travel Society on 9th September 1960. Its destination was Eastleigh, and it was hauled by Midland Compound No. 1000 from Nottingham Victoria to Oxford and return, and is seen before departure from Nottingham. *Gavin Morrison*

The classic pairing of the Midland Compound and No. 5690 *Leander* produce a breathtaking sight near Wortley Junction as they leave Leeds for Harrogate and York on 20th October 1979.

Gavin Morrison

No. 5000 passes through tranquil Shropshire countryside near Onibury on 23rd October 1982 with a northbound "Welsh Marches Pullman".

John Whiteley

No. 5305 *Alderman A.E. Draper* accelerates away from Skipton heading for Carlisle on a special which it worked from Leeds on 8th March 1986.

John Whiteley

No. 5593 *Kolhapur* finds a patch of brilliant afternoon sunshine as it leaves Appleby after a photo stop on its way from Leeds to Carlisle on 21st March 1987.

John Whiteley

A mid-week southbound run over the Settle and Carlisle line on 3rd July 1980 was hauled by No. 5690 *Leander* seen making spectacular progress through Dent.

John Whiteley

The handsome lines of No. 6201 *Princess Elizabeth* are seen to full advantage in this picture taken on 24th October 1987 as she nears Ludlow in the autumnal sunshine.

John Whiteley

No. 777 *Sir Lamiel* (30777)

In 1918 the first of 20 of Robert Urie's N15 class 4-6-0s emerged from Eastleigh Works for express passenger use on the London & South Western Railway. By the Grouping all 20 of these engines were engaged primarily on the Waterloo-Exeter route via Salisbury.

After the formation of the Southern Railway in 1923, its Chief Mechanical Engineer, R. E. L. Maunsell, selected the design of the N15s for further construction with various improvements and modifications, and a further 54 were built between 1925 and 1927 including No. E777 *Sir Lamiel* which was built by the North British Locomotive Company in June 1925. The "E" prefix to the number signified an LSWR engine and was removed when the Southern Railway implemented its renumbering scheme in 1931. All the N15s were given names from the Arthurian legends and they soon became known as the 'King Arthur' class.

Initially No. E777 *Sir Lamiel* was allocated to Nine Elms, and before long the 'King Arthurs' were proving to be very versatile engines and were hard at work over most of the Southern system. By the mid-1930s they were at the zenith of their achievements and in 1936 No. 777 *Sir Lamiel* achieved some notoriety whilst working the up "Atlantic Coast Express" when it cut $17^1/4$ minutes from the booked time of 90 minutes for the 83.8 miles from Salisbury to Waterloo, with a maximum speed of 90mph at Byfleet.

Sir Lamiel was transferred to the Eastern Section for a time and was shedded at Dover, but after completion of the first stage of the Kent Coast electrification was transferred back to the Western Section, being withdrawn as BR No. 30777 from Basingstoke in October 1961. No. 30453 *King Arthur* was initially earmarked for preservation, but in the event *Sir Lamiel* was selected for official preservation as part of the National Collection and spent several years in store at various places. Eventually, in June 1978 it was moved from the National Railway Museum to the Humberside Locomotive Preservation Group in Hull for restoration to main line running condition in its pre-war guise.

The re-appearance of *Sir Lamiel* on the main line was one of the highlights of 1982. Its first outing was northbound over the Settle and Carlisle line on 27th March 1982, but it was not allowed to work the train on its own and "Black Five" No. 5407 was put inside to provide additional power if required. The pair are seen at Keld, nearing Appleby, with the return southbound "Cumbrian Mountain Pullman" on 3rd April 1982. *Sir Lamiel* was allowed to do most of the work which appears to be resulting in a glowing smokebox door.

John Whiteley

On 4th December 1982 No. 777 *Sir Lamiel* is erupting from Appleby with the southbound "Cumbrian Mountain Pullman". During 1982 *Sir Lamiel* was used extensively on the main line, based at Carnforth or York and put up some very creditable performances.

John Whiteley

A magnificent trail of back-lit exhaust hangs almost motionless in the cold and still morning air of 27th December 1984 at Settle Junction as *Sir Lamiel* rushes past on a Leeds-Appleby section of a "Santa Steam Special".

John Whiteley

This picture clearly illustrates how the addition of smoke deflectors can significantly alter the appearance of a locomotive, not always for the better. The 'King Arthurs' were originally built without deflectors and for a short spell *Sir Lamiel* ran in this state. On 6th July 1986 it is seen accelerating away from a slack in Harbury Cutting with the "Shakespeare Limited" returning from Stratford upon Avon to Marylebone.

Pete Skelton

No. 841 *(Greene King)* (30841)

The story of the development of the S15 class 4-6-0s is very similar to that of the N15s, in as much as the S15s were also designed by Robert Urie for the London & South Western Railway and subsequently improved by Maunsell when he was appointed CME of the Southern Railway at the 1923 Grouping.

The S15 was designed by Urie as a goods engine, and although similar in appearance to the N15 had 5ft 7in coupled driving wheels, unlike the 6ft 7in of the N15. These 20 Urie S15s appeared from Eastleigh Works between March 1920 and May 1921, and when a more powerful main line freight locomotive was required by the Southern Railway later in the 1920s Maunsell did not produce a new design, but merely re-introduced the Urie S15 design with his own modifications, and a further 15 were built at Eastleigh during 1927 and early 1928. The final batch of 15 S15s were all built at Eastleigh in 1936, including No. 841, which appeared in July, and these were the last new large engines constructed during Maunsell's term of office.

Whilst built primarily for goods services and proving to be very capable engines, they were often pressed into service on passenger turns, and even allowing for their relatively small 5ft 7in coupled wheels, gave an excellent account of themselves. They were associated with Feltham shed but were a familiar sight on the heavy Western Section goods turns working from Salisbury and Exmouth Junction sheds. Withdrawal of the S15s did not commence until 1962 and they outlived the 'King Arthurs', some still being in regular use in 1965. No. 30841 was withdrawn from Feltham shed in January 1964 and also found the haven of Woodham's Barry scrapyard. It was rescued from there by the Essex Locomotive Society in 1972, restored to working order as SR No. 841 in green livery and named *Greene King*. It made only brief appearances on the main line in the late 1970s, but can now be seen working regularly on the North Yorkshire Moors Railway, still as SR No. 841, but now in plain black livery.

No. 841 *Greene King's* inauspicious main line outings were confined to East Anglia, and sadly were plagued with difficulties. On the murky morning of 3rd April 1976 it is seen near Claydon, shortly after leaving Ipswich, with the Manningtree-March steam section of an excursion from Liverpool Street to Loughborough.

L.A. Nixon

No. 850 *Lord Nelson* (30850)

Heralded as the most powerful express locomotive in the country, No. E850 *Lord Nelson* appeared from Eastleigh Works in August 1926, following demands from the Southern Railway authorities for a locomotive capable of hauling 500 ton trains at an average speed of 55mph. Although the 'King Arthurs' were performing admirably, they were not up to the demands of the increasing loads of these faster trains, particularly on the Eastern Section with the heavily-loaded Continental boat trains.

The prototype was monitored closely for some time and its results evaluated before a further ten four-cylinder 'Lord Nelsons' were ordered from Eastleigh in lieu of ten 'King Arthurs'. These all appeared during 1928 and 1929 and a final five appeared late in 1929, making a total of 16 in all. The 'Lord Nelsons' were soon working not only on the Eastern Section but elsewhere on the Southern, which could have led to their disappointing performances as neither drivers nor firemen were working with them on a regular basis and were therefore unfamiliar with their characteristics.

Various modifications were made to certain members of the class in an attempt to improve their performance, but it was not until the arrival of Bulleid as CME of the SR in 1937 that the problem of poor steaming was solved. He carried out alterations to blastpipe and chimney arrangements and finally fitted a Lemaitre multiple jet exhaust and wide chimney to No. 863 *Lord Rodney*. This was considered a success and all 16 engines had been similarly dealt with by the end of 1939. No. 850 *Lord Nelson* was rebuilt in this manner in June 1939 and it is now preserved in this form. It was during this immediate pre-war period that the 'Lord Nelsons' were producing the best performances of their careers and from February 1940 the whole class was allocated to Nine Elms. After the arrival of the Bulleid Pacifics the 'Lord Nelsons' tended to be relegated to secondary passenger duties and were later concentrated at Eastleigh, working Southampton boat trains and Waterloo-Bournemouth trains. They were also used on some inter-regional trains between Bournemouth and Oxford, and although working semi-fasts to Salisbury from Waterloo, they were rarely to be seen west of Salisbury.

They were all withdrawn during 1961 and 1962, *Lord Nelson* being withdrawn in August 1962. After withdrawal and being earmarked as part of the National Collection it spent long periods in store at various places in Southern territory, finally moving to Steamtown at Carnforth in 1976 after a brief spell at the National Railway Museum. It was restored to working order in SR malachite green livery and in May 1980 was steamed for the first time in 18 years. It participated in the Rainhill celebrations of 1980 and has since been a regular main line performer.

The massive proportions of No. 850 *Lord Nelson* can be seen in this photograph as it drifts effortlessly along the shores of Morecambe Bay at Meathop, near Grange-over-Sands. It is heading "The Lancastrian" special on the section from Carnforth to Sellafield on Bank Holiday Monday 25th August 1980.

John Whiteley

On 20th June 1981 No. 850 is near Guide Bridge en route from Northwich to Leeds with the "Yorkshire Pullman" special.

Gavin Morrison

Heading a southbound "Cumbrian Mountain Express" on 11th September 1983 *Lord Nelson* is steaming towards New Biggin.

Gavin Morrison

In pouring rain *Lord Nelson* is near Kettles-beck Bridge on the Carnforth-Skipton leg of the northbound "Cumbrian Mountain Express" on 15th November 1980.

John Whiteley

To commemorate the 150th anniversary of first transporting troops by rail in the UK, a steam special was run on Wednesday 11th March 1981 between Liverpool and York hauled by *Lord Nelson*, seen here between Dewsbury and Batley.

John Whiteley

Still a long way from native Southern territory, No. 850 is near Soulby on the Settle and Carlisle line on 29th July 1981 heading the "Wedding Belle", so named because of the wedding of HRH Prince Charles on the same day.

Gavin Morrison

No. 35028 *Clan Line*

When Maunsell retired as CME of the Southern Railway in 1937 he was replaced by O.V.S. Bulleid who had been assistant to Gresley from 1911 on first the GNR and then the LNER, interrupted only by a four year spell during the First World War. Bulleid took over at a time when the SR's steam power was at a fairly low ebb, a considerable amount of investment having been devoted to electric traction. One of his first achievements was to improve the performance of the 'Lord Nelsons' by improved front end and exhaust alterations, but his experience on the LNER was clearly to have a bearing on what was to follow on the Southern.

Bulleid had been closely associated with the design of the Gresley 2-8-2s for the difficult Edinburgh-Aberdeen line and at one stage considered a similar 2-8-2 wheel arrangement for the Southern which, as it happened, was not readily accepted by The Civil Engineer. In the event a design of 4-6-2 wheel arrangement was conceived which had distinct similarities to the Gresley 2-8-2 at the front end, incorporating as it did smoke deflectors as an integral part of the boiler casing. Such was the appearance of the 'Merchant Navy' Pacific which emerged from Eastleigh in June 1941, at a difficult time during the Second World War.

Authority had been given in 1938 for ten new main line steam locomotives which were required to haul 550-600 ton trains at an average speed of 60mph on the Eastern Section and 70mph on the Western Section. Design work was delayed by the outbreak of war but when the first one did appear it was of an unorthodox appearance, described as air-smoothed, and in that respect certainly very different from the Gresley designs. It was a three-cylinder engine, with 6ft 2in driving wheels and a total of 20 appeared from Eastleigh between 1941 and June 1945, with the odd Bulleid

numbering system of Nos 21C1–21C20. A third and final batch of ten 'Merchant Navys' appeared from Eastleigh in the early days of Nationalisation, including in December 1948 No. 35028 which was named *Clan Line* in the following October.

Although there were detail differences in these later engines it became obvious that despite their free steaming characteristics, their air-smoothed casing and other unconventional features made them costly to maintain, and a decision was therefore taken by BR in 1955 to modify them. No. 35018 *British India Line* was the first to undergo modification and it appeared from Eastleigh in February 1956 with distinct external similarities to the Riddles BR Standard engines. All 30 'Merchant Navys' were rebuilt in this manner, No. 35028 *Clan Line* being the last, in October 1959, prior to which it had been a regular performer on the "Golden Arrow" and "Night Ferry" turns whilst based at Stewarts Lane. Once rebuilt the 'Merchant Navys' were more reliable engines and still capable of high speed running. After rebuilding and completion of the first stage of the Kent Coast electrification the 'Merchant Navys' were transferred to the Western Section where they went out in a blaze of glory, often reaching speeds in the region of three figures.

The last members of the class ended up at Nine Elms and Weymouth on the last steam worked main line in Britain which finally gave way to modernisation in July 1967. *Clan Line* was officially withdrawn on 9th July 1967 having covered almost 800,000 miles in service and far from life-expired. It was purchased by the Merchant Navy Locomotive Preservation Society and after a brief spell of storage at Nine Elms was successfully steamed again at Longmoor and subsequently moved to Ashford and then Bulmers at Hereford.

On 29th September 1984 No. 35028 *Clan Line* lifts a northbound "Welsh Marches Express" bound for Chester effortlessly out of Shrewsbury, past the remains of Coton Hill Yards.
John Whiteley

Running neck and neck with a dmu, but banked at the rear by a Class 25 diesel, *Clan Line* climbs Miles Platting Bank out of Manchester Victoria on 21st June 1980 with a special, taking it back to Hereford.
Gavin Morrison

On 15th September 1979 *Clan Line* is leaving Sheffield on its way to Shrewsbury and Hereford with a train, aptly titled "The Strongbow Express".

John Whiteley

Resplendent in sparkling BR green livery and carrying all the "Golden Arrow" embellishments, No. 35028 is seen climbing effortlessly past Fosse Road on 19th October 1986 and catching the last rays of the late afternoon sun, as it hurries a Sunday excursion back to Marylebone from Stratford upon Avon.

John Whiteley

No. 34092 *City of Wells*

Following the introduction of his revolutionary 'Merchant Navy' Pacifics, Bulleid designed a scaled-down version intended for use on the many SR secondary routes, where the 21 ton axle-loading of the 'Merchant Navys' was restricted. These light Pacifics had an axle-loading of 18 tons 15cwt, and were essentially similar in appearance to the 'Merchant Navys' and were intended for use on both passenger and goods trains, primarily in the West of England. Hence the SR decided to call these new light Pacifics the 'West Country' class and name them appropriately. A total of 110 light Pacifics were built between 1945 and 1951, of which 44 became known as the 'Battle of Britain' class, although they were identical to the 'West Countrys'.

No. 34092 was completed at Brighton Works in October 1949 and having run unnamed for a few weeks was named *Wells* on 25th November 1949 at a ceremony at Wells in Somerset. In April 1950 this was altered to *City of Wells* and new nameplates were duly fitted by BR. It was allocated to Stewarts Lane shed at Battersea and was a regular sight at the head of the expresses between London Victoria and the Channel ports. It was obviously one of the most outstanding of the light Pacifics and spent long periods working the prestige "Golden Arrow" Pullman trains during the 1950s. This was one of the most exacting duties for a Stewarts Lane engine which was invariably turned out in spotless condition with embellishments consisting of 15ft long side arrows for the locomotive side and ornate headboard at the front, together with twin flags above the bufferbeam.

No. 34092 remained at Stewarts Lane until electrification of the Eastern Section when it was moved to Salisbury in June 1961 to complete its days on the Western Section. Whilst there its original 5,500 gallon tender was exchanged for a cut-down 4,500 gallon tender which had formerly been attached to No. 34051 *Winston Churchill*. It was withdrawn from Salisbury in November 1964 after the South Western lines of the Southern Region were taken over by the Western Region and dieselised. After a career of only 15 years and having run approximately 502,000 miles *City of Wells* went to the Barry scrapyard from where it was purchased privately for restoration to working order on the Keighley & Worth Valley Railway in Yorkshire. Restoration took eight years and *City of Wells* is now beautifully preserved in BR Brunswick green livery, never having carried SR Malachite green and never having been rebuilt by BR like the 'Merchant Navys' and some of the other light Pacifics had been. It is now a regular performer on both the Keighley & Worth Valley Railway and also the main line, on which it has made many very commendable runs.

In the spring of 1986 No. 34092 *City of Wells* was fitted with a Giesl Oblong Ejector and it is clearly seen in this picture as it leaves Leeds with the "Pennine Limited" to Appleby on 2nd July 1986.

John Whiteley

Complete with all the "Golden Arrow" embellishments and newly fitted Giesl Ejector, No. 34092 is approaching Rodley on 3rd June 1986 soon after leaving Leeds with a press trip for the forthcoming summer Settle and Carlisle excursions that used steam haulage between Leeds and Appleby.

Gavin Morrison

City of Wells made a welcome return to main line running in 1981, since when it has distinguished itself on many occasions. In sub-zero temperatures of 12th December 1981 it is passing Kettlesbeck Bridge, again with "Golden Arrow" finery. Its intended run was from Carnforth to Leeds and return, but due to operating difficulties caused by the severe weather earlier in the day, the train was running very late and it returned to Carnforth from Skipton in order to make up time.

John Whiteley

The first trip of No. 34092 over the arduous gradients of the Settle and Carlisle line was in February 1982, and it is seen here on 13th February 1982 on its first southbound journey from Carlisle, crossing Long Marton Viaduct with the "Cumbrian Mountain Pullman".

John Whiteley

Only rarely is it possible to photograph preserved steam at Ais Gill in the morning with the sun on the east side, but on 26th September 1987 an excursion to York organised by Appleby Round Table made a very early departure from Carlisle. It made a marvellous sight approaching the summit behind *City of Wells* with early morning cloud partly obscuring the top of Wild Boar Fell.

John Whiteley

Ex-LMS Engines

No. 123

Although the famous Caledonian Single No.123 was built in 1886 during the eight year term Dugald Drummond was Locomotive Superintendent of the Caledonian Railway, it was designed and built privately by Neilson & Co., but with obvious Drummond characteristics. Only one of these 4-2-2s was built, specifically for display at the Edinburgh International Exhibition of 1886, and it had 7ft driving wheels with two inside cylinders. It was taken into Caledonian Railway stock as No. 123 after closure of the Exhibition and commenced work on the main lines of the CR,

participating in the "Races to the North" of 1888. In 1914 it was placed on the "duplicate list" as No. 1123 but was renumbered 14010 by the LMS and ended its days on the Perth-Dundee line, by then the last "single" in Britain in revenue earning service, finally being withdrawn in 1935. It was stored for some time at St Rollox but finally emerged in 1958 restored to working order as No. 123 in its splendid Caledonian blue livery. Initially it worked some specials in connection with the Scottish Industries Fair of 1959, but continued to work periodically until 1965 when it was retired to the Glasgow Museum of Transport as a static exhibit.

A splendid sight on 12th May 1962 as Caledonian No. 123 and No. 256 *Glen Douglas* steam towards Dalmally at the head of Loch Awe as they return to Glasgow from Oban with an SLS special.

Gavin Morrison

On 14th September 1959 No. 123 pilots "Jones Goods" No. 103 at Partick West with empty stock of an excursion from Renfrew Wharf to Glasgow Kelvin Hall during the Scottish Industries Fair.

J.G. Dewing

Prior to returning to Glasgow on 12th May 1962 No. 123 is seen on the turntable at Oban.
Gavin Morrison

Another view of No. 123 and *Glen Douglas* returning from Oban to Glasgow on 12th May 1962. The pair are passing the summit at Glenoglehead before dropping steeply down Glenogle on a spectacular stretch of line which was closed prematurely in September 1965. This was due to a rock slide in Glenogle causing trains to use the ex-NBR route to Crianlarich via Arrochar.

Gavin Morrison

No. 790 *Hardwicke*

Of the constituents of the LMS in 1923, by far the greatest motive power contribution came from the London & North Western Railway, both in terms of actual numbers of locomotives and also advanced passenger locomotive designs. It is a pity, therefore, that more LNWR locomotives have not been preserved. However, as part of the National Collection No. 790 *Hardwicke* has survived in its original condition. It was one of 166 Webb 'Precedent' class 2-4-0s which were built between 1874 and 1901 – the "Jumbos" as they became known. They had 6ft 9in coupled driving wheels and participated in the main express passenger workings on the "Premier Line" until the introduction of the larger 4-4-0s and 4-6-0s in the 1910 period.

Hardwicke achieved fame in August 1895 during the "Races to the North" when there was intense rivalry between the operators of the East and West Coast routes to Scotland, initially to Edinburgh in 1888 and then to Aberdeen in 1895 after the opening of the Forth Bridge. On 22nd August 1895 *Hardwicke* worked the West Coast train between Crewe and Carlisle in a record time, and this record remained intact until November 1936 when it was broken by No.6201 *Princess Elizabeth*, as described later in this book.

Only 80 of these "Jumbos" were in service at the Grouping, the first one having been withdrawn in 1908. The last one survived until 1934, *Hardwicke* having been withdrawn as LMS No. 5031 in 1932.

For a spell during 1976 No. 790 *Hardwicke* was based at Carnforth and worked a series of trains to Grange-over-Sands. In May of that year it is seen shortly after leaving Carnforth.
John Whiteley

A portrait taken at York shed yard on 24th April 1976, prior to *Hardwicke* and Midland Compound No. 1000 working a Gainsborough Model Railway Society special to Carnforth.
Gavin Morrison

A picture which emphasizes how locomotive proportions changed between the pre-Grouping and post-Nationalisation periods as both train loads and speeds increased. Is *Hardwicke* pulling or being pushed by No. 92220 *Evening Star* on 19th June 1976 as they cross Clapham Common with the LCGB "Fells and Dales" railtour.

Gavin Morrison

Another slightly bizarre combination of motive power on 8th May 1976 as *Hardwicke* and No. 4472 *Flying Scotsman* approach Plumpton Junction near Ulverston with a special from Carnforth to Sellafield.

John Whiteley

On the following day *Hardwicke* is leaving Grange-over-Sands with a four-coach shuttle to Carnforth.

John Whiteley

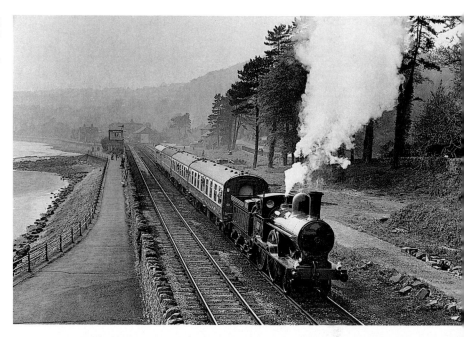

No. 1054 (58926)

Another LNWR locomotive to survive is 2F class 0-6-2T No. 1054. This was also designed by Francis William Webb during his term as Locomotive Superintendent of the LNWR from 1871 to 1903. A total of 300 were built at Crewe between 1881 and 1896 and these "Coal Tanks", as they became known, were introduced primarily for use on freight traffic. However, they were very versatile and equally at home on light passenger workings, many of them push-pull fitted for this purpose.

The majority of the "Coal Tanks" came into LMS ownership at the 1923 Grouping, and 64 survived Nationalisation, including No. 1054 which became BR No. 58926. It was the very last LNWR tank engine when it was withdrawn in 1958 and after withdrawal it was acquired by the National Trust and restored as LNWR No. 1054, and later maintained in main line running order by the Dinting Railway Centre. Its main line outings have been limited, but it was a very popular attraction at both the Keighley & Worth Valley Railway and the Severn Valley Railway when it made brief visits to each in 1986.

On a very dismal 18th October 1986 No. 1054 leaves Chester with an SLS special from Shrewsbury to Stockport celebrating the 80th birthday of enthusiast Mr W.A. Camwell.
Gavin Morrison

After a very successful visit to the Keighley & Worth Valley Railway, Webb "Coal Tank" No. 1054 is seen emerging from Thackley Tunnel on 1st August 1986 on its return journey to Dinting.

D. Phillips

On 28th May 1980 No. 1054 pauses at Manchester Victoria in the company of a dmu on its return from the "Rocket 150" celebrations at Bold, to its base at Dinting.

Gavin Morrison

Another view of No. 1054 working back to Dinting on 1st August 1986. It has just emerged from Gledholt Tunnel on the climb out of Huddersfield.

D. Phillips

No. 103

When William Stroudley moved to the London, Brighton & South Coast Railway in 1870, David Jones was appointed Locomotive Superintendent of the Highland Railway which had been formed in 1865. Jones held that position for 26 years and towards the end of his career was responsible for the introduction of his "Big Goods" which was the first engine of a 4-6-0 wheel arrangement in Britain. Such was the confidence of the Highland Railway in the designs of Jones that 15 of these engines were ordered straight off the drawing board. They were all built in 1894 by Sharp, Stewart & Co, at a cost of £2,795 each, the first one, No. 103 appearing in September 1894. They soon became known as the "Jones Goods" and were at the time of their introduction the heaviest locomotives in the country and rated as the most powerful. They were an immediate success working heavy goods trains over the Highland main line and the experience gained from these excellent locomotives helped David Jones and his successors to develop express passenger 4-6-0s.

No. 103 spent time allocated to both Inverness and Perth and was renumbered 17916 by the LMS after the Grouping. The "Jones Goods" continued to do good work on the Highland Section under LMS ownership but withdrawal commenced in 1929, although the last one survived in service until early 1940. The pioneer engine was withdrawn in July 1934 and was set aside by the LMS for preservation. Initially it was stored at St Rollox and was restored during 1935 and 1936 as HR No. 103 in green livery. In 1959 it was restored to working order for the Scottish Industries Exhibition and painted in the Stroudley "improved engine green" which was essentially a dark yellow which later became better known as "Brighton yellow" on the LBSCR. After working a variety of trains for a few years it was retired to the Glasgow Museum of Transport in 1965, from where hopefully it may eventually re-emerge to work special trains.

The "Jones Goods" No. 103 is seen in all its splendour at Holbeck motive power depot, Leeds, on 25th May 1964. It was returning to Scotland after taking part in the filming of "Those Magnificent Men in their Flying Machines", part of which was filmed in the Bedford area.

Gavin Morrison

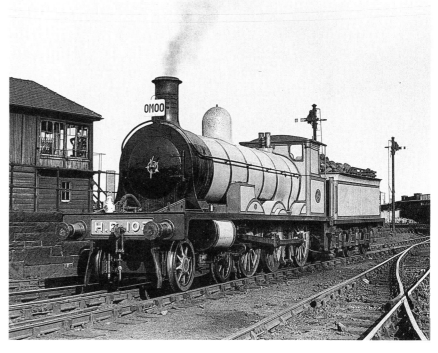

On home territory, No. 103 is seen leaving Perth on 21st August 1965 heading for Inverness with a train composed of two former Caledonian Railway coaches, prior to working a week of exhibition runs between Inverness and Elgin to celebrate the centenary of the Highland line.

J.R.P. Hunt

No. 80 *Thundersley* (41966)

In 1912 the London, Tilbury & Southend Railway was absorbed by the Midland Railway and by the 1923 Grouping 70 of the 94 engines of LT&SR origin, which were included in MR, stock were Atlantic tank engines. One of these was class 3P 4-4-2T No. 2177 which was designed by Thomas Whitelegg for the LT&SR and built in 1909. It was originally LT&SR No. 80 *Thundersley,* as now preserved, but it was renumbered 2177 by the MR and its name removed. *Thundersley* was one of four of these handsome Atlantic tanks which were built in 1909, twelve earlier engines being rebuilt to the same design. A further 35 engines were built by the LMS between 1923 and 1930, and in 1930 No. 2177 was renumbered 2148, finally renumbered 41966 by BR.

It spent most of its life working London suburban services, initially on the LT&SR between Fenchurch Street and Southend via Upminster or Tilbury and latterly on the Midland lines from St Pancras. Although the LMS built engines survived in service until 1960, *Thundersley* was the last LT&SR engine to be withdrawn, in 1952, and has been preserved in its original colours and can now be seen at the Bressingham Steam Museum in Norfolk.

Superbly restored in LT&SR colours, No. 80 *Thundersley* poses at Bishopsgate on 11th February 1956 before departure with the RCTS "Southend Centenary Special".

W.M.J. Jackson

Seemingly being raced by a flock of pigeons No. 80 departs from Bishopsgate on 11th February 1956.

W.M.J. Jackson

The LT&SR coat of arms.

C.R.L. Coles

As part of the London, Tilbury & Southend Railway centenary celebrations a special was run behind *Thundersley* on 3rd March 1956 from Southend to Liverpool Street. It proved to be a very wet day and the train is seen passing Pitsea.

W.M.J. Jackson

L.T. & S.R. Centenary
SOUTHEND
TO
BISHOPSGATE
FIRST CLASS
1st to 17th March, 1956

Arriving at Liverpool Street on 3rd March 1956 with an ex-LT&SR coach next to *Thundersley* which can also be seen in the previous pictures. Although restored for this occasion the coach was subsequently broken up.

C.R.L. Coles

No. 1000 (41000)

In January 1902 No. 2631, the pioneer Midland Compound, appeared from Derby. It was renumbered 1000 in 1907 and was the first of five compound 4-4-0s built for the Midland Railway during 1902 and 1903 to meet the need for more powerful locomotives to deal with heavier trains. It was designed by Johnson to Smith's compound design with one high pressure cylinder inside the frames and two low-pressure cylinders outside. Between 1905 and 1909 Deeley built a further 40 compound 4-4-0s and the original five engines were rebuilt between 1914 and 1919 to this later Deeley design. It is in this rebuilt Deeley form that No. 1000 is now preserved. Deeley was succeeded by Henry Fowler, and although a further 195 Compounds were built under the Fowler regime, they did not appear until after the Grouping and the formation of the LMS in 1923. They were soon working all over the LMS system but when the LMS finally embarked upon its big-engine policy they tended to be relegated to more secondary duties, particularly after the introduction of Stanier's "Black Five" 4-6-0s.

The Midland Compounds all had 7ft diameter driving wheels and right hand drive, but the LMS Compounds had 6ft 9in driving wheels and apart from the first 40, had left hand drive. Until the application of plain black livery after the Second World War they had run in crimson lake livery, but after Nationalisation they were repainted in lined-black BR mixed-traffic livery.

Withdrawal of the Compounds commenced in 1948 and the last of the Midland Compounds was withdrawn early in 1953. As BR No. 41000, the pioneer Midland Compound was withdrawn in October 1951, but the last of the LMS Compounds was not withdrawn until 1961. No. 41000 remained in Crewe Works for some time after withdrawal, but in 1959 it re-emerged for working special trains having been painted in MR crimson lake as part of the National Collection. For a time it was displayed at the British Transport Museum in Clapham before being transferred to the National Railway Museum at York, from where it periodically works on the main line.

It is doubtful that a pairing of a Midland Compound and an LNER V2 class 2-6-2 ever occurred in steam days, either before or after Nationalisation, but on 3rd May 1980 the colourful combination is passing through Rodley Cutting shortly after leaving Leeds on the way to Carnforth.

John Whiteley

On 5th October 1981 Midland Compound No. 1000 was employed on a private charter train for Ford Motor Company executives. Immaculately turned out it is leaving York at the start of its journey to Harrogate, Leeds and back to York.

John Whiteley

The classic combination of No. 1000 and No. 5690 *Leander* are making steady progress south on the Settle and Carlisle line, having just passed Armathwaite with a southbound "Cumbrian Mountain Pullman" on the wintry day of 12th February 1983.

John Whiteley

The pairing of No. 1000 and No. 4771 *Green Arrow* first occurred on 26th May 1979 when they worked "The Curator" railtour which was organised to commemorate the death of Mr John Scholes, the former Curator of the National Railway Museum. The pair are climbing towards Chinley, near the site of Gowhole Yards, on their way to York.

Gavin Morrison

No. 13809/53809

Henry Fowler (Sir Henry Fowler from January 1918) was appointed Chief Mechanical Engineer of the Midland Railway in 1910. Apart from pursuing the MR "small engine" policy as far as passenger locomotive requirements were concerned, he was confronted with the need for larger and more powerful locomotives to replace the medium size 0-6-0s on the heavy mineral trains of the Somerset & Dorset Joint Railway. The Midland Railway was responsible for the locomotives of the S&DJR and in 1914 six handsome 2-8-0 outside-cylinder freight engines were built at Derby specifically for use on the S&DJR. In 1925 a further batch of five locomotives was built by Robert Stephenson & Co. Ltd. to meet the demand for additional motive power on the line, and this batch included No. 89 which was to become LMS No. 9679 in 1930, No. 13809 in 1932 and finally No. 53809 in 1948. This second batch of 2-8-0s differed from the 1914 engines by having a larger non-standard boiler, but had few other modifications and was turned out in the standard plain black livery which all these 2-8-0s retained throughout their existence.

No. 89 was involved in a serious accident at Bath in 1929 and was returned to traffic from Derby with the smaller standard boiler of the original batch. Another one of the last batch was similarly dealt with shortly afterwards, but the other three were not reboilered until 1953/5.

Apart from being loaned very briefly to the MR in 1931 and having previously been used briefly on trials against ex-LNWR 0-8-0s and ex-MR 0-6-0s, these 2-8-0s were associated exclusively with the S&DJR for which arduous route they were ideally suited.

Although introduced as freight engines, having a coupled wheel diameter of 4ft 8$\frac{1}{2}$in, after Nationalisation they were often pressed into use on passenger turns, particularly on busy summer Saturdays when they could sometimes be seen double-heading with a variety of different locomotives. Seldom, however, did these 7F class 2-8-0s work in pairs on passenger trains.

The first of the class to be withdrawn was in 1959 and No. 53807 was the last to remain in service, being withdrawn in September 1964. No. 53809 was withdrawn in June 1964, and tragically the line itself closed on Sunday 6th March 1966 after the Western Region had transferred away the majority of traffic and reduced it to little more than a country branch line. Fortunately No. 53809 ended up at Barry, and after eleven years was rescued from there by Mr Frank Beaumont and restored to working order by a dedicated group of enthusiasts. Restoration was completed at Butterley, the headquarters of the Midland Railway Centre where it is currently based.

The eagerly awaited return of No. 13809 to the main line occurred on 2nd May 1981 when it hauled a special from Guide Bridge to York and return. Reviving memories of the Somerset & Dorset it is depicted climbing slowly from Chinley North Junction to Cowburn Tunnel on the outward journey.

John Whiteley

On 27th March 1982 No. 13809 passes Bentham on the Carnforth-Hellifield section of a northbound ''Cumbrian Mountain Pullman''.

Gavin Morrison

The 7Fs rarely saw quadruple tracks during their working lives, but on 2nd May 1981 No. 13809 passes Bolton Percy on its way to York.

John Whiteley

Having been repainted in BR livery, No. 53809 is seen working a train to Ludgershall from Andover on 27th October 1987 as part of the Basingstoke Rail Week celebrations, formed somewhat incongruously of Network SouthEast stock.

Pete Skelton

No. 6115 *Scots Guardsman* (46115)

When the London Midland & Scottish Railway Company came into being in January 1923 it was the largest of the "Big Four" and inherited over 10,000 steam locomotives of almost 400 different types. Sir Henry Fowler was appointed Chief Mechanical Engineer of the LMS in 1925, following the retirement of George Hughes, Fowler having been CME of the Midland Railway from 1910 until the Grouping. It was not really surprising therefore that the Midland Railway became the dominating influence within the LMS, despite the fact that the LNWR had contributed not only more locomotives but more advanced designs to the LMS group.

The MR "small engine" policy was initially perpetuated by the LMS which inevitably led to a considerable amount of double-heading of the heavier trains, but by late 1926 a larger locomotive was required for the following summer's timetable when it was proposed to introduce a new train for the Anglo-Scottish route which was beyond the capability of any existing LMS engine to work without double-heading. Fifty new three-cylinder 4-6-0s were therefore ordered straight off the drawing board. The order was given to the North British Locomotive Company at Glasgow and the first of the 'Royal Scots' appeared in July 1927, the remainder all being delivered by November of the same year. No. 6115 was completed in September 1927 and named *Scots Guardsman* in 1928. The design was so successful that a further 20 'Royal Scots' were built at Derby in 1930.

By the time some of the 'Royal Scots' had been in service for ten years and more, boilers were due for renewal and several locomotives were suffering from cracked frames and leaking smokeboxes. A decision was therefore taken to modify them with Stanier taper boilers and double chimney, William Stanier having taken over as CME of the LMS in 1932. The first of those "Converted Royal Scots" appeared in 1943, but bearing in mind that very little of the original Fowler engine was retained, the description "Rebuilt Royal Scot" is more appropriate and is generally used. *Scots Guardsman* was rebuilt in 1947 and was the first of the rebuilt locomotives to be fitted with smoke deflectors, and it is in this condition with post-war LMS express black livery with maroon and straw lining that it is now preserved.

Withdrawal of the 'Royal Scots' commenced in 1962 and *Scots Guardsman* was the last to remain in traffic, being withdrawn in January 1966 from Carlisle Kingmoor. It was purchased for preservation and initially went to the Keighley & Worth Valley Railway, subsequently moving to the Dinting Railway Centre where it was painstakingly restored to main line running order.

Another view of the "Yorkshire Venturer" sees *Scots Guardsman* climbing towards Chinley on 11th November 1978.

John Whiteley

Resplendent in its post-war LMS lined black livery, No. 6115 *Scots Guardsman* is nearing Chinley North Junction on 11th November 1978 on its journey from Guide Bridge to York with the "Yorkshire Venturer" railtour.

John Whiteley

Shortly before its first public main line outing No. 6115 undertook a test run from Guide Bridge to Sheffield on 21st September 1978. Although restoration work had been almost completed, it ran without its tender having been repainted, and is seen here climbing out of Sheffield on the return journey.

John Whiteley

Although its return to the main line had been eagerly awaited, sadly it was not to last for long. *Scots Guardsman* was only passed by BR to work two public main line trains during 1978, and 11th November 1978 proved to be its last outing until major boiler repairs have been carried out. A trip over the Settle and Carlisle line with a rake of maroon coaches is, as yet, a pipe dream! It is seen here near Chinley North Junction.

Gavin Morrison

No. 6201 *Princess Elizabeth* (46201)

Soon after the introduction of the 'Royal Scots' the LMS was faced with the need for an even larger and more powerful locomotive capable of working 500 ton expresses between Euston and Glasgow. William Stanier had been "poached" from the GWR and appointed Chief Mechanical Engineer of the LMS on 1st January 1932 and one of his first designs was a Pacific to meet this requirement. No. 6200 *The Princess Royal* was completed at Crewe in June 1933 and was soon followed by No. 6201 which left Crewe Works in November 1933 and shortly afterwards was officially named *Princess Elizabeth*.

Initially three prototype Pacifics were ordered, but in the event the third appeared in 1935 as a non-condensing turbine locomotive – No. 6202 the "Turbo-motive" as it became known. Ten more conventional 'Princess Royals' appeared from Crewe during 1935 while No. 6202 was later rebuilt by BR as near to a conventional 'Princess Royal' Pacific as possible, appearing in June 1952 as No. 46202 *Princess Anne,* but tragically it was destroyed on 8th October 1952 in the Harrow & Wealdstone disaster.

No. 6201 *Princess Elizabeth* cost £11,675 to build, £2,465 over the authorised cost of £9,210 for each of the first two Pacifics, and was allocated to Camden. No. 6201's "finest hour" came in November 1936 when it was involved in a return non-stop test run between Euston and Glasgow on the 16th and 17th to assess both the needs of the high-speed services planned for 1937

and also the capabilities of the 'Princess Royals'. On the northbound journey the 401.4 miles was covered in 353 min 38 sec, a gain of over six minutes on the original schedule which itself was 105 minutes faster than the schedule of the 'Royal Scot'. Southbound the following day the run took just 344 min 15 sec with one extra coach, eight coaches in all. The times achieved by *Princess Elizabeth* have never been improved upon by steam traction.

In common with the other 'Princess Royals' No. 6201 was painted in crimson lake livery when new and subsequently was repainted in two separate styles of black, one LMS and one BR, and finally BR Brunswick green. The locomotive was shedded at Camden, Polmadie, Longsight, Edge Hill, Crewe North, Carlisle Kingmoor and finally Carlisle Upperby from where it was withdrawn in October 1962, having covered just over 1 1/2 million miles.

The second phase of its career began in February 1963 when it was purchased from BR by the Locomotive 6201 Princess Elizabeth Society Ltd, a fund having been started in October 1961. Initially it was based at Ashchurch, where restored to working order in LMS livery with the domed boiler which was originally fitted when new to No. 6203, and the Stanier 10 ton capacity tender which was fitted in November 1936. In April 1976 *Princess Elizabeth* moved to Bulmer Railway Centre, Hereford from where it commenced regular main line running.

April 24th 1976 marked the return of *Princess Elizabeth* to the main line when she deputised for No. 6000 *King George V*. She is seen here leaving Hereford for Chester on 5th June 1976 on her first society railtour – the "Sir W.A. Stanier Centenary Special" train, complete with "703" headboard, as carried on the record run of November 1936.

John Whiteley

Opposite: Regarded by many, including the photographer, as one of the finest locomotives ever to grace BR metals, No. 6201 *Princess Elizabeth* makes a characteristic sure-footed departure from Craven Arms on 24th October 1987 on an outing from Swindon to Shrewsbury via Gloucester and Newport.

John Whiteley

On her return to service after a lengthy overhaul at Hereford, *Princess Elizabeth* is seen climbing majestically towards Diggle on 15th November 1986 with a heavy thirteen coach train, steam hauled between Stockport and Carnforth.

John Whiteley

Princess Elizabeth has seen a considerable amount of work on the North and West route since preservation, and on 11th April 1981 is shown passing the site of St Devereux station with a southbound "Welsh Marches Express".

John Whiteley

Gleaming in the late afternoon sun of 15th November 1986, No. 6201 is accelerating a special away from Settle Junction on the way to Carnforth.

John Whiteley

Running through the attractive Shropshire countryside near Ludlow, *Princess Elizabeth* is depicted heading a special from Swindon to Shrewsbury on 24th October 1987.

John Whiteley

No. 5593 *Kolhapur* (45593)

By the early 1930s the Fowler parallel boiler 'Royal Scots' were handling a lot of the principal express passenger trains of the day, but there was a need for an intermediate main-line passenger locomotive which could operate over routes from which the larger 'Royal Scots' were barred. Fowler had already rebuilt two of the LNWR 'Claughtons' prior to introduction of the 'Patriots' which were in a sense scaled down 'Royal Scots', but William Stanier, newly appointed CME of the LMS, took the opportunity to include five new taper boiler 5XP class 4-6-0s in the reviewed 1932 locomotive construction programme.

Design work commenced in 1932 and the first orders were placed during 1933 for no fewer than 113 of these new three-cylinder 4-6-0s to be built in four separate batches, two at Crewe, one at Derby and one by the North British Locomotive Co. The first batch of five, Nos 5552 – 5556 were completed at Crewe during the spring of 1934. In April 1935 No. 5552 was named *Silver Jubilee* (having exchanged identities with No. 5642) and henceforth the class was referred to as 'Jubilees' and not 5XP.

No.5593 was built by the North British Locomotive Co. at their Queens Park Works in December 1934 and was later named *Kolhapur*. During 1935 and 1936 a further 78 'Jubilees' were built at Crewe, making a total of 191 which was the most numerous class of six-coupled express passenger engine built by the LMS.

It is fair to say that the 'Jubilees' were not an immediate success and suffered initially from poor steaming, but after Stanier had modified the boiler design and increased the superheating their performance improved considerably. For 30 years they were a familiar sight on most lines of the LMS and later London Midland Region of British Railways, often roaming beyond. They became associated with the Settle and Carlisle line but did not see regular service on either the former Highland or Somerset & Dorset sections.

Amongst other sheds, *Kolhapur* was allocated to Longsight and Carlisle Upperby, but ended up at Leeds Holbeck and by the summer of 1967 was one of only three 'Jubilees' remaining in traffic, working regularly over the Settle and Carlisle line. It was finally withdrawn in October 1967 when it was purchased and restored to working order at the Birmingham Railway Museum, Tyseley, in its original LMS red livery.

The locomotive has successfully just managed to elude the sun as No. 5593 comes off Lunds Viaduct on 22nd March 1987 on its way to Carlisle, with a "Cumbrian Mountain Express'.

John Whiteley

No. 5593 *Kolhapur* made a welcome return to main line running in 1985, and on 8th June it is seen making its debut run on the "Shakespeare Express" between Hall Green and Stratford upon Avon in attractive rural surroundings near Wythall, climbing towards Earlswood Lakes.

Pete Skelton

On 25th April 1987 *Kolhapur* is seen climbing Ashwood Dale towards Buxton with a train from Derby.

J.R.P. Hunt

No. 5593's return to the Settle and Carlisle line was on 22nd March 1987 with a "Cumbrian Mountain Express" which it worked between Leeds and Carlisle. With a sprinkling of snow lying in places it is forging towards Horton-in-Ribblesdale.

John Whiteley

Earlier in the day *Kolhapur* is nearing Gargrave on its way from Leeds to its stop at Long Preston for water.

John Whiteley

Photographic run pasts have become common practice and to the delight of onlookers *Kolhapur* puts on a spectacular display at Appleby.

John Whiteley

No. 5596 *Bahamas* (45596)

No. 5596 *Bahamas* was also built by the North British Locomotive Co., at their Queens Park Works, and was completed in January 1935. Trials had been conducted on a few 'Jubilees' from the late 1930s using a Kylchap double blastpipe and chimney arrangement and although never regarded as particularly successful, similar trials recommenced in the mid-1950s. *Bahamas* was fitted with this arrangement as late as 1961 which is rather surprising as by this time the days remaining for steam locomotives were running out and little development work was being done.

With the mass introduction of diesels in the early 1960s the 'Jubilees' were being demoted to secondary passenger duties and were often to be seen on freight working. Large numbers of withdrawals commenced in 1962 and by the mid-1960s the class had been decimated. *Bahamas* was withdrawn from Stockport Edgeley in July 1966 as BR No. 45596, still with its double chimney, and was purchased by the Bahamas Locomotive Society. It was given a major overhaul by the Hunslet Engine Co. and is now based at the Dinting Railway Centre. It was restored to LMS livery, but still with its double chimney which it never had in LMS days.

No. 5596 *Bahamas* had only a brief spell of main line duty in the early 1970s, and on 14th October 1972 it bursts out of Ludlow Tunnel on the way to Newport from Shewsbury.
John Whiteley

On 17th June 1973 *Bahamas* worked a special from Guide Bridge to Sheffield, and late in the afternoon it is seen on the return train climbing out of Sheffield past the disused carriage sidings near Millhouses. The locomotive has now been repainted in BR green, which is the correct livery for its double chimney status.

No. 5690 *Leander* (45690)

Unlike the other two preserved 'Jubilees' which were both built by the North British Locomotive Co., No. 5690 *Leander* was built at Crewe, and appeared during March 1936. *Leander* was amongst the final Crewe built 'Jubilees', all of which were constructed with improved boilers with separate dome and top feed, unlike the earlier examples which were rebuilt in a similar manner at a later date.

Four different types of tender were attached to the 'Jubilees' when they were first built, and *Leander* was fitted with the later Stanier 4,000 gallon type, as now preserved. After delivery *Leander* was allocated to Crewe, but following nationalisation spent most of its time allocated to Bristol Barrow Road working primarily on the Bristol-Birmingham-Sheffield-Leeds-York route. It was withdrawn from Bristol Barrow Road in March 1964 and was sold to Woodham's for scrap. After spending nine years in their Barry scrapyard it was purchased privately and restored at the Derby Works of British Rail at great expense. It subsequently spent time at both Dinting and Steamtown, Carnforth and is currently based on the Severn Valley Railway where further boiler and mechanical repairs were carried out to main line standards.

'Jubilees' were no strangers to the ex-Glasgow & South Western, and displaying a "Thames-Clyde Express" headboard No. 5690 *Leander* is steaming through the picturesque Drumlanrigg Gorge on 20th April 1985 on its way from Kilmarnock to Carlisle.

Gavin Morrison

Some of the finest work of the 'Jubilees' was done on the Settle and Carlisle line, and on 3rd July 1980 *Leander* is seen passing through Kirkby Stephen station with a southbound "Cumbrian Mountain Express".

John Whiteley

On 26th April 1980 No. 5690 heads south towards Lazenby, at Baron Wood, on a special which it hauled from Hellifield to Carlisle and return.

John Whiteley

A 'Jubilee' can generally be relied upon to give a lively and often noisy performance. March 13th 1982 was certainly no exception, and the footplate crew seemed to be enjoying themselves as *Leander* positively roared past Dorrington on the long climb out of Shewsbury with a southbound "Welsh Marches Pullman."

John Whiteley

Even in 1980 the landscape around Blea Moor Tunnel was in the process of being disfigured by forestry, as can be seen in this picture taken on 26th April. It shows *Leander* emerging from Blea Moor Tunnel with the "Leander Enterprise" special to Carlisle.

John Whiteley

No. 5025 (45025)

Soon after the 1923 Grouping the LMS was faced with the need for "an engine that would go anywhere and do anything", and this was still high on the list of priorities for Stanier in 1932. An engine was needed which could operate over virtually the whole of the LMS system and which was capable of use on express passenger trains and branch line freight alike. Such a design was intended to replace numerous ageing pre-Grouping engines and the initial order to Crewe for 20 was followed immediately by a contract with Vulcan Foundry for a further 50. Although the numbers 5000–5019 were allocated to the Crewe engines, the Vulcan Foundry engines appeared first and these had been allocated the numbers 5020–5069. No. 5025 appeared from Vulcan Foundry in August 1934 and in common with all early engines originally had a domeless boiler.

These mixed-traffic engines were originally classified 5P5F, but subsequently amended to simply Class 5. They were turned out in black livery, unlike the red three-cylinder 'Jubilees', and were originally referred to as "Black Staniers", later "Black Fives". These two-cylinder taper boiler engines were soon producing outstanding performances and construction proceeded steadily until Stanier retired in 1944. The design was perpetuated by both Fairburn and H. G. Ivatt, until by the early years of Nationalisation when the last one appeared in May 1951, a total of 842 had been built, ten fewer than Stanier's 8Fs.

The "Black Fives" proved to be one of the most versatile and successful classes of locomotive ever built and it is not surprising that several survived until steam was finally eliminated from regular service on BR in August 1968.

No. 5025 spent part of its life working in Scotland, particularly on the Highland line, and with this in mind it was purchased privately from BR after withdrawal as No. 45025 in August 1968 for use on the planned Strathspey Railway. Although it spent its early years of preservation on the Keighley & Worth Valley Railway, it moved to the Strathspey Railway in 1975 where it can still be seen.

After an absence of 20 years, steam returned to the Kyle line in 1982 in the shape of No. 5025 which worked a private charter on 29th May 1982. Later in the year, on 25th September, it worked the first public excursion, the "Ravens Rock Express" from Inverness to Kyle of Lochalsh, and it is seen here on that day skirting the beautiful Loch Carron near Attadale.

J.R.P. Hunt

On 6th July 1981 No. 5025 was used on the Highland main line when it hauled an excursion from Perth to Aviemore and is seen here passing the distillery at Dalwhinnie on the outward journey.

John Whiteley

With a Class 37 diesel for company, No. 5025 is preparing to leave Inverness on its first public run to Kyle of Lochalsh on 25th September 1982.

J.R.P. Hunt

Following its run on 25th September, No. 5025 worked private charter train for the Toyota Car Company on four consecutive days from 4th to 7th October. On 5th October it is seen leaving Achnasheen on its scenic journey to Kyle of Lochalsh.

J.R.P. Hunt

No. 5000 (45000)

No. 5000 was the first engine of the first batch of 20 "Black Fives" ordered from Crewe, and it appeared in February 1935. Although No. 5000 was intended to be the first of the class to appear, it was not, somewhat embarrassingly, simply because Vulcan Foundry completed the engines of their first batch earlier than Crewe and No. 5020 had been the first to appear in August 1934. No. 5000 was built with a domeless boiler and was initially allocated to Crewe North. It spent its entire working life on the "North Western" section and was withdrawn in October 1967, having been selected for preservation as part of the National Collection. It was stored at various places for several years and was finally entrusted to the Severn Valley Railway in 1977 for restoration, since when it has worked on both the main line and the Severn Valley Railway very successfully.

On 30th January 1982 No. 5000 worked the first of the 1982 season's "Welsh Marches Pullman". Not surprisingly it is making heavy weather of the long climb out of Shrewsbury, near All Stretton, with a twelve coach train.

John Whiteley

The "Welsh Dragon" special was double-headed by Nos 5000 and 43106 from Shrewsbury to Newport and back to Hereford. The pair are leaving Shrewsbury at Sutton Bridge Junction in the rain on 11th October 1980.

John Whiteley

No. 5305 *Alderman A.E. Draper* (45305)

Armstrong Whitworth built a total of 327 "Black Fives" in two separate batches, and No. 5305 was included in the second batch of 227, appearing in January 1937. The sanctioned cost of locomotive and tender in this batch was £6,080 each and they were all delivered with domed boilers with improved superheating, unlike the first 225 "Black Fives" which had been built in five separate batches at Crewe, Vulcan Foundry and Armstrong Whitworth. Prior to the outbreak of the Second World War, the "Black Fives' were painted black with a single red lining to the boiler, firebox, cab-sides, running plate and cylinder casing, some also having a single red line round the cab windows. The first 225 engines had shaded scroll and serif numerals and letters, but the second batch built by Armstrong Whitworth, were given the then new sans serif numerals and letters with red shading, in which livery No. 5305 is now preserved.

No. 5305 was initially allocated to Carnforth and spent most of its life in the North of England being withdrawn from Lostock Hall, near Preston, in August 1968 as BR No. 45305. It was bought for scrap by Mr. A.E. Draper of Hull who subsequently decided to restore it to working order. The Humberside Locomtoive Preservation Group was formed and in 1976 No. 5305 was again steamed at Dairycoates shed, Kingston upon Hull. From 1977 it has been a regular performer on the main line, still based at Hull in the care of the Humberside Locomotive Preservation Group, and is now named *Alderman A. E. Draper*.

No. 5305 worked a private charter from Hull to Chester and back on 18th April 1981 and is seen leaving an unusually empty York station on the outward journey.

John Whiteley

Right: After its season working between Fort William and Mallaig No. 5305 was permitted to work a train south over the West Highland main line on 17th October 1987. On the spectacular stretch of line between Bridge of Orchy and Tyndrum Upper it is climbing away from Horseshoe Curve.

John Whiteley

Overlooked by the splendid Chester No. 2 signal box, No. 5305 leaves with the return train to Hull on 18th April 1981.

John Whiteley

Below: Now named *Alderman A. E. Draper* No. 5305 is near Arisaig on 10th June 1987 heading for Mallaig during a very successful season working from Fort William. It is hauling the "Royal Scotsman" luxury train on its scenic tour of Scotland. The first three coaches are worthy of mention. First is the Observation Car (CR No. 41) which was built in 1892, originally used as a dining car, but converted to an observation car by the Caledonian Railway for use on the North Highland line. Second is the Saloon Car (GNR No. 807) built in 1912 for The Great Northern Railway and third, the Dining Car (LNWR No. 5159) built in 1891 for use on London-Manchester expresses.

J. R. P. Hunt

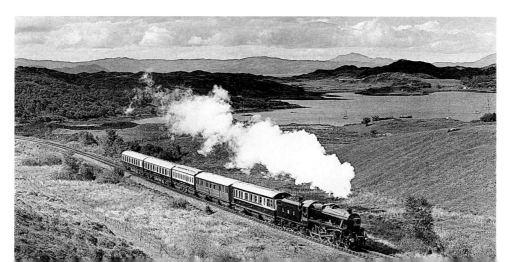

No. 5407 (45407)

No. 5407 was also in the second batch built by Armstrong Whitworth, and appeared in September 1937. It was also amongst the last "Black Fives" in service and was finally withdrawn from Lostock Hall, Preston, in August 1968 having given over 30 years faithful service. It was purchased privately and restored to BR livery as No. 45407 at Steamtown, Carnforth and worked various main line specials during the mid 1970s. For a brief period in 1970 it was painted in Furness Railway red livery, but in 1980 it was repainted in LMS black livery as No. 5407. Since then it has participated in a considerable number of main line specials, notably on the West Highland line from Fort William to Mallaig.

On 27th May 1984, No. 5407 is climbing towards Glenfinnan with the "West Highlander" on its way from Fort William.

J. R. P. Hunt

On 29th April 1978 a pair of 'Black Fives' are leaving York with a train returning to Carnforth. No. 45407 in BR black livery is leading No. 44932 in lined green livery.

John Whiteley

No. 5407 climbs towards Giggleswick on 28th March 1981, now repainted in LMS black livery and heading the "Cumbrian Mountain Express" on the steam section from Hellifield to Carnforth.

John Whiteley

No. 5407 has also participated in working between Fort William and Mallaig. On 4th August 1985 it is shown leaving Mallaig with the "West Highlander".

J. R. P. Hunt

No. 5407 had the distinction of hauling the first steam hauled train on the scenic Mallaig Extension of the West Highland line on 27th May 1984 after an absence of steam for over 20 years. It is seen here on its historic first day of revenue earning service passing through magnificent scenery as it skirts the end of Loch Eilt heading for Mallaig.

J. R. P. Hunt

No. 44871 *Sovereign*

A total of 472 Black Fives had been completed by the end of 1938 and due to other wartime needs no more were ordered until 1943, when 35 were ordered from Derby. Before the end of the war Derby, Crewe and Horwich were all building "Black Fives" and No. 4871 was included in a batch built at Crewe, and appeared in March 1945. Before the appearance of No. 4871 the number 5499 had been reached by the class, and as the later 'Patriot' 4-6-0s already commenced with the number 5500, numbering of "Black Fives" was restarted at 4800. After Nationalisation 40000 was added to the numbers of LMS locomotives and No. 4871 became BR No. 44871 in December 1949. The first "Black Five" was withdrawn in 1961 following collision damage, but regular withdrawal began in 1962. By the beginning of 1968 only approximately 150 were left in service and No. 44871 was one of the final survivors, all being concentrated in Lancashire.

On Sunday, 11th August 1968, one week after the end of normal steam working on BR, a special was run by BR from Liverpool and Manchester to Carlisle and back and three "Black Fives" were involved, including No. 44871 which piloted No. 44781 on the return from Carlisle to Liverpool. After withdrawal it was preserved in BR livery at Steamtown, Carnforth and is now named *Sovereign*.

On one of its few main line outings No. 44871 *Sovereign* is piloting No. 45407 near Bentham on a train from Carnforth to Leeds on 24th September 1977.

Gavin Morrison

No. 44932

No. 4932 was the first "Black Five" to be completed at Horwich, and appeared in September 1945. It was included in a small batch which were sanctioned at a cost of £9,500 each for locomotive and tender, £3,000 more than the first Crewe built "Black Fives" of 1935. By the time No. 4932 appeared from Horwich, C. E Fairburn was CME of the LMS, having taken over from Stanier in 1944. Fairburn continued with construction of the "Black Fives", unchanged, but he died suddenly in October 1945 and was succeeded by H. G. Ivatt who was to introduce some modifications to the "Black Fives" and also some experimental versions.

No. 4932 was renumbered 44932 in April 1949 and was withdrawn in August 1968. It was preserved at Steamtown, Carnforth, and initially repainted in lined green livery. Subsequently it moved to the Midland Railway Centre at Butterley and was repainted in early BR black livery.

The lined green livery of No. 44932 can be seen in this picture of its leaving Skipton on 29th April 1978. It is being piloted by No. 45407 on a train from Carnforth to Leeds.

Gavin Morrison

Now repainted in early BR lined black livery, No. 44932 is leaving Fort William on 1st September 1986 with the "West Highlander" to Mallaig. Since the return of steam in 1984 to the Mallaig Extension, two engines have been based at Fort William during the season to work the services, and during 1986 No. 44932 was sharing the work with No. 44767.

J. R. P. Hunt

Canal locks dominate this picture of No. 44932 taken on 3rd November 1985 near Burscough when it was working tender first on a Wigan–Southport excursion as part of a Festival of Nostalgia sponsored by a Southport newspaper.

L. A. Nixon

No. 4767 *George Stephenson* (44767)

H. G. Ivatt was appointed CME of the LMS in January 1946 following the unexpected death of Fairburn. Problems of locomotive servicing and maintenance had been highlighted during the difficult wartime years and Ivatt immediately introduced modifications to the basic Stanier design in an attempt to improve matters. The first post-war bulk order for 65 "Black Fives" included self-cleaning smokeboxes, rocking grates and self-emptying ashpans. Several of these engines also incorporated other modifications, including No. 4767 which was built with outside Stephenson link motion, Timken roller bearings throughout, electric lighting and double chimney. It appeared from Crewe as the last new LMS locomotive, entering service on 31st December 1947 at a cost of £13,278 and was renumbered 44767 in April 1948. Due to problems with drifting exhaust obscuring the driver's forward vision the double chimney and twin exhaust were replaced by a single chimney in 1953 and the electric lighting apparatus was removed at about the same time.

No. 44767 spent its working life based in the North West and was withdrawn from Carlisle Kingmoor in December 1967. After a spell at Steamtown, Carnforth, it was purchased by Mr Ian Storey and restored to main line running condition in time for the Shildon celebrations in 1975 where it was named *George Stephenson*. This unique "Black Five" has seen a considerable amount of main line running and is still a regular performer on the North Yorkshire Moors Railway.

Deputising for No. 673 *Maude* on 13th April 1985, No. 44767 is passing Forteviot on its way to Perth open day with an excursion from Falkirk.

Gavin Morrison

To mark the 200th anniversary of the birth of George Stephenson special trains ran between Newcastle and Hexham behind No. 4767 on 6th June 1981. One of these is near Blaydon alongside the River Tyne, seemingly at low tide, on its way to Hexham.

John Whiteley

After the **BR** open day, No. 44767 is seen leaving Perth and accelerating its featherweight train towards Moncrieff Tunnel on the return to Falkirk.

John Whiteley

A classic "Black Five" and 'Jubilee' combination in the shape of No. 44767 and No. 5690 *Leander* leaving Blackburn on 23rd February 1985 on their way from Manchester Victoria to Carlisle.

Gavin Morrison

Another picture of one of the anniversary specials of 6th June 1981. No. 4767 leaves Hexham for Newcastle with the splendid NER signal box and signals in evidence.

John Whiteley

On 4th April 1981 No. 4767 double-heads with No. 5407 on the Settle and Carlisle line. The pair are approaching Armathwaite with a northbound "Cumbrian Mountain Express".

John Whiteley

No. 48151

By the time Stanier came to the LMS in 1932 both the GWR and LNER were running large numbers of 2-8-0s capable of handling heavy freight traffic, but the LMS was still relying largely on 2-6-0s and 0-6-0s. It was only to be expected, therefore, that Stanier would produce a 2-8-0 heavy freight engine for the LMS and this emerged from Crewe in 1935 in the shape of No. 8000 which was a two-cylinder, taper boiler engine which incorporated many features of his earlier "Black Five". This was one of the initial batch of twelve locomotives which were classified 7F, later to be classified 8F in line with later examples which were built with improved boilers.

Subsequent batches were built, mainly at Crewe, and they were soon working efficiently on the lines of the LMS. Not surprisingly, they were chosen as the Ministry of Supply freight locomotive for wartime service and orders were placed with various builders, including railway company workshops at Swindon, Horwich, Doncaster, Brighton and Eastleigh, until a total of 852 had been built by the end of the war, making it numerically the largest Stanier class. Of these, 133 were pure War Department owned and never carried LMS numbers, and a considerable number never returned to British soil after the war, either being destroyed or ending up in such places as Turkey, Egypt and Iraq.

The 8Fs wandered far and wide on BR after Nationalisation and underwent relatively few modifications. They could not only be seen on freight workings but also empty stock workings and often passenger service on busy summer Saturdays. In their latter days all the survivors were concentrated in the North of England and they became famed for their duties on the ICI limestone trains from Tunstead to Northwich. The last few were finally withdrawn on 4th August 1968, the last day of regular steam on BR.

No. 8151 was built at Crewe in 1942 and did not see wartime service overseas. After it was withdrawn as BR No. 48151 it ended up in the Barry scrapyard. It remained there for many years before being purchased in 1975 by Mr David Smith, a Wakefield businessman. It moved from Barry to the Yorkshire Dales Railway at Embsay in November 1975, but little restoration work had been done by 1979 when it was moved to Wakefield. There it was restored in its BR livery, but major boiler repairs were carried out at Butterley, following which it appeared at the Crewe Heritage Exhibition in 1987. Now based at Butterley, the first BR fare-paying special it worked was when it deputised for No. 4472 *Flying Scotsman,* and has made several appearances on the main line since. Perhaps the most notable of these were a number of "Blackmore Vale Express" trains in July 1988.

On its first main line outing No. 48151 leaves Chesterfield in spectacular fashion heading for Buxton on its way from Derby, 24th October 1987.

John Whiteley

No. 46229 *Duchess of Hamilton*

In the mid-1930s the streamlining of trains and locomotives was very much the fashion and although the 'Princess Royals' were performing well on the Anglo-Scottish route, an improved Pacific design was needed. It is not surprising therefore that Stanier introduced the first of these new Pacifics in streamlined form.

The first five of these streamlined locomotives, Nos 6220–6224, appeared from Crewe in June and July 1937, all painted in a striking rich blue livery with silver lining along the sides, commencing in a chevron at the front of the locomotive. A special high speed train between Euston and Glasgow was introduced in 1937, named the "Coronation Scot" and turned out in the same eye-catching livery as the first five streamlined Pacifics which were to haul the train. No. 6220 was named *Coronation*, the class becoming known as the 'Princess Coronation' class. Five more were built during 1938, including No. 6229 *Duchess of Hamilton*, also in streamlined form but in maroon and gilt livery, presumably to blend better with the standard LMS maroon carriages when they were not working the "Coronation Scot" but on ordinary express passenger use. Twenty-eight more 'Princess Coronation' Pacifics were built between 1938 and 1948, the first five non-streamlined, the next fourteen streamlined and the final nine non-streamlined.

The 'Princess Coronation' Pacifics were Stanier's last design for the LMS and considered by many to be his masterpiece. The first 15 "Duchesses", as the 'Princess Coronations' came to be known, had single chimneys, but the remainder were all built with double chimneys, earlier engines being similarly modified later, including *Duchess of Hamilton*, in April 1943. Difficulty maintaining the streamlined engines during the war prompted the decision to remove the exterior casings from all the 24 which were so built, and *Duchess of Hamilton* was de-streamlined in November 1947 when smoke deflectors were added. It is now preserved in this condition as BR No. 46229 in BR red livery which it first received in 1958, in common with 15 other "Duchesses", all based on the London Midland Region.

Disregarding the streamlining of some, the "Duchesses" differed from the earlier 'Princess Royals' by having an improved and larger boiler, slightly larger coupled driving wheels of 6ft 9in diameter and simplified valve gear. This resulted in an outstandingly successful design, so much so that No. 6220 *Coronation* immediately set a new speed record for steam traction of 114mph on the special press run of the new "Coronation Scot" in June 1937, only to be broken by the 126mph of the LNER's No. 4468 *Mallard* the following year.

Climbing at 1 in 100 but still with steam to spare on a thirteen coach train, No. 46229 *Duchess of Hamilton* has just crossed Smardale Viaduct with a southbound "Cumbrian Mountain Express" on 28th March 1981.

John Whiteley

Duchess of Hamilton changed identities with No. 6220 *Coronation* in 1939 and was shipped to North America for the New York World's Fair, unable to return until 1943 because of wartime conditions. On its return it resumed its former identity as No. 6229 and recommenced work on the West Coast Main Line notching up just over 1½ million miles before being withdrawn in February 1964. Tragically the mass withdrawal of the remaining 19 "Duchesses" occurred in September 1964, the majority still in excellent mechanical condition. However, *Duchess of Hamilton* was acquired for static display at one of Butlin's Holiday Camps and was subsequently loaned to the National Railway Museum in York and restored to working order, largely at the expense of the Friends of the National Railway Museum. For some of us who thought that steam had in effect come to an end in September 1964 when these mighty engines were withdrawn, it is a delight to see *Duchess of Hamilton* on the main line once again. Sadly, however, never again shall we see her on Shap or Beattock where the magnificent spectacle of a "Duchess" in full flight will best be remembered by both authors.

On 11th November 1980 No. 46229 accelerates away from Marsh Lane Cutting, Leeds, with a train from Liverpool to York to commemorate 150 years of transporting mail by rail. Next to the engine is the preserved LNWR royal brake No. 5155 and behind that a travelling post office van.

John Whiteley

With patchy snow lying on the northern hills, *Duchess of Hamilton* pounds majestically towards Blea Moor on the way from Leeds to Carlisle on 26th March 1983 with a train which originated at Sheffield.

Gavin Morrison

No. 46443

After the railways were nationalised in 1948 H. G. Ivatt remained as CME, but he was only responsible for London Midland Region locomotive affairs. When he retired in June 1951 as the last of the CMEs of the former "Big Four" companies, the title of CME lapsed. The first of his three designs for the LMS was a Class 2 mixed-traffic 2-6-0 with the emphasis upon ease of maintenance and operation. They were introduced to replace some of the pre-Grouping types still being used on secondary services and soon proved to be ideal for branch line duties and other light work. The first 20, Nos 6400–6419, were built at Crewe before Nationalisation and so successful were they that further construction was authorised by the Railway Executive after Nationalisation.

Further batches were built at Crewe, Darlington and Swindon between 1948 and 1953 for use on the London Midland, Eastern, North Eastern and Western Regions of British Railways, until a total of 128 were in service. No. 46443 was built at Crewe in 1950 and incorporated improved draughting after tests had been carried out at Swindon after Nationalisation, between a Dean goods 0-6-0 and Ivatt 2-6-0 No. 46413. With their tender cabs and inset coal bunkers these Ivatt Moguls were popular with footplate crews and proved to be economical yet lively performers. However, with the onset of dieselisation they were destined to have a short working life on BR and the last members of the class were all withdrawn during 1967. To date seven have been spared the cutter's torch and No. 46443 is preserved on the Severn Valley Railway where it can be seen regularly working between Bridgnorth and Kidderminster, and from where it has made periodic main line outings.

In 1987 No. 46443 participated in some of the Cambrian workings, and on 31st August it is passing alongside the Dovey Estuary near Aberdyfi with a train heading for Machynlleth.
D. Phillips

On 26th September 1987 a series of shuttles were run between Birmingham Moor Street and Knowle & Dorridge to mark the closure of Moor Street station. No. 7029 *Clun Castle* was also used, but No. 46443 is seen here on one of the trains, having just passed Tyseley.
John Whiteley

As part of the GW150 celebrations trains were run between Bristol Temple Meads and Portishead. Although not a GWR locomotive, the fact that some of these Moguls were built at Swindon must have been sufficient reason to allow No. 46443 to participate. It is leaving Temple Meads in June 1985 with the "Avon Gorge" special to Portishead.

Pete Skelton

Some of the Ivatt Moguls did work on the former Cambrian lines, so No. 46443 does not look entirely out of place leaving Dovey Junction for Machynlleth on 1st September 1987 complete with "Cardigan Bay Express" headboard.

D. Phillips

No. 43106

Ivatt's third and final design for the LMS was the 4F mixed-traffic 2-6-0 which was developed as a modern replacement for the numerous ageing inside-cylinder 0-6-0 goods engines. Later classified 4MT, only three appeared before Nationalisation, Nos 3000–3002, but by 1952 a total of 162 had been built at Horwich, Doncaster and Darlington. The desire for ease of maintenance resulted in a high running plate and the austere appearance of these Moguls was not enhanced by the large and rather ugly double chimney which was fitted to the first 50 when built.

Despite all their modern features, in service they were poor steamers, and after tests had been carried out all the double-chimney engines were fitted with a single chimney. When draughting problems were finally solved after tests at Swindon these Moguls settled down to give very satisfactory service.

No. 43106 was built at Darlington and was completed in April 1951. Initially it was allocated to South Lynn working over the former Midland & Great Northern Joint Lines. It then moved to the ex-Great Central section before seeing service at Saltley, Wellingborough, Kettering, Trafford Park, Heaton Mersey, Carlisle Kingmoor and finally Lostock Hall from where it was withdrawn in June 1968. The 4MT was purchased by a group of Severn Valley Railway members and has been based at Bridgnorth ever since. A far cry from the impressive early designs of the LMS produced by Fowler and Stanier, and often referred to as "Flying Pigs" or "Flying Bedsteads" due to their ungainly appearance, No. 43106 has nevertheless performed admirably both on the Severn Valley Railway and on its rather infrequent main line outings.

Deputising at short notice for No. 5593 *Kolhapur*, on 11th April 1981 No. 43106 worked solo with a train from Dorridge to Didcot and it is seen here approaching Heyford.

Gavin Morrison

Another view of No. 43106 heading the SVR railtour of 11th April 1981 which originated at Manchester. It is seen here accelerating the eight coach special away from Banbury on the return journey from Didcot.

Gavin Morrison

A pair of SVR locomotives are leaving Hereford on 26th February 1983. Nos 80079 and 43106 are working the steam section from Hereford to Newport and return, having taken over from No. 4930 *Hagley Hall* at Hereford on the southbound "Welsh Marches Pullman".

John Whiteley

On 11th April 1981 No. 43106 meets a southbound express headed by Class 47 No. 47485 near Culham, on its way back to Dorridge from Didcot.

Gavin Morrison

LNER Group Locomotives

No. 1

Patrick Stirling was the second Locomotive Superintendent of the Great Northern Railway and held that position from 1866 until he died in office on 11th November 1895. He came to Doncaster from the Glasgow & South Western Railway, and although a degree of standardisation was introduced by him, the familiar lines of the Doncaster locomotives for the GNR soon appeared.

Without doubt his most famous design was his 4-2-2, referred to as the eight-foot single because of the diameter of the driving wheels. The first of these was No. 1 which was built at Doncaster in 1870 and was the first of a long line of Stirling singles which were constructed until 1894. These eight-foot singles were very successful locomotives and handled principal GNR expresses in the late Victorian era. They were involved in the famous "Races to the North" of 1888 when the booked journey time of the 10 o'clock morning train from King's Cross to Edinburgh was progressively cut from 9 hours to 7³/4 hours.

No. 1 was based at Doncaster for its entire working life and was withdrawn in 1907 after being displaced from the premier express passenger workings of the day by the larger and more powerful Ivatt Atlantics. Following withdrawal it was preserved with the intention of displaying it as a static exhibition piece, but in 1938 it was restored to working order by the LNER at the time they were advertising new rolling stock for the non-stop "Flying Scotsman" express from London to Edinburgh. After a brief spell of main line running in 1938, it was transferred to York Railway Museum where it remained until 1975 when it was transferred to the new National Railway Museum at York as a prominent exhibit in the Main Hall. To the delight of enthusiasts, in late 1981 it was restored to working order and worked on the Great Central Railway for a few weeks under the supervision of the late John Bellwood, the then CME of the NRM. After its return to York it visited the North Yorkshire Moors Railway briefly for filming purposes, but can again be seen sporting its splendid GNR green livery in the Main Hall of the NRM, serving as an evocative reminder of the Victorian era of our railways.

On one of the famous specials in 1938, GNR No. 1 is seen near Potters Bar with the RCTS excursion from King's Cross to Peterborough on 11th September. It was unfortunate that a 'down' express overtook the special at the crucial point!

C. R. L. Coles

No. 673 *Maude* (65243)

Sadly very few locomotives built by the North British Railway survive, but one that does is No. 673 *Maude*. It was designed by Matthew Holmes who was Locomotive Superintendent of the North British Railway for 21 years from 1882 until 1903, succeeding Dugald Drummond who moved to the Caledonian Railway and later the London & South Western Railway.

Holmes continued with the general Drummond tradition of design, but he also embarked upon a programme of rebuilding some of the older engines to current standards and introduced new designs with larger boilers and increased boiler pressures. One of these new designs, introduced in 1888 was his NBR Class C 0-6-0 goods engines which had 5ft coupled wheels and a boiler pressure of 165lbs. The Class C was a development of his earlier Class D 0-6-0 and altogether a total of 168 of these successful Class C 0-6-0s were built during a 13 year period, including No. 673 *Maude* which was built in 1891.

Reclassified J36 by the LNER, *Maude* was one of 25 of the class which was transported overseas during the First World War and saw service in France. In common with the other 24, No. 673 was given a name with wartime connections when it returned to Scotland in 1919 after its spell abroad.

All 168 of these very useful 0-6-0s were in service at the Grouping and the vast majority were still in service at Nationalisation. As BR No. 65243 *Maude* was withdrawn in July 1966 and was acquired by the Scottish Railway Preservation Society at Falkirk and restored by them to main line running order.

On a fine sunny morning near the start of what was probably one of its longest workings ever, from Kilmarnock to Bold Colliery in Lancashire, No. 673 nears Polquhap Summit on the Glasgow & South Western main line on 17th May 1980.

John Whiteley

Maude leaves Falkirk Grahamston for Larbert, sporting the 'Rainhill' celebration headboard, on 4th May 1980.

John Whiteley

The present day main line preservation scene usually involves large locomotives. However, NBR No. 673 *Maude* is probably the most notable exception as it has travelled frequently around Fife and the Edinburgh area on a number of specials. It has also ventured onto the Fort William–Mallaig line, as well as a memorable trip from Kilmarnock over the Settle and Carlisle line to the Rocket 150 celebrations. On 4th May 1980 in its fine North British lined black livery it is seen leaving Haymarket.

John Whiteley

Dwarfed by the mighty Forth Bridge, *Maude* blows off as it approaches North Queensferry on 4th May 1980.

John Whiteley

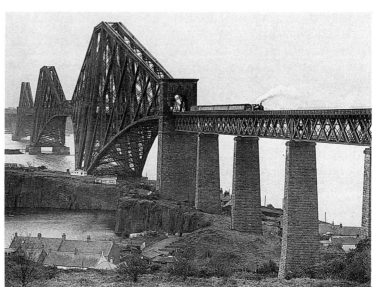

Battling against a strong east wind, slow progress is being made by No. 673 on the climb from Inverkeithing to North Queensferry on 4th May 1980.

Gavin Morrison

No. 1247 (68846)

Henry Alfred Ivatt was appointed Locomotive Superintendent of the Great Northern Railway in March 1896 following the death of Patrick Stirling in November 1895. The 0-6-0T was generally considered by the GNR to be the most suitable type for shunting duties, and both Stirling and Ivatt produced a long line of saddle tanks of this wheel arrangement. In August 1897 Ivatt introduced the first of 85 Class J13 0-6-0Ts which were a development of Ivatt's earlier Class J14. All the earlier J14s were subsequently rebuilt to Class J13 and were reclassified J52 by the LNER.

No. 1247 was built in May 1899 and was one of 25 built by Sharp, Stewart & Co. It was renumbered 4247 by the LNER, later 8846 and finally 68846 by BR in 1948. The J52s were concentrated mainly at the large marshalling yards and were an integral part of the scene around London with both King's Cross and Hornsey having large allocations. Intensive withdrawals of J52s began in 1951 and No. 68846 was one of the last two remaining in London when it was withdrawn in May 1959. Ardsley was the final shed to play host to J52s when the last one was withdrawn in March 1961.

When No. 68846 was withdrawn it was purchased by Captain W. G. Smith and restored to its former GNR livery. Initially it was kept at Marshmoor near Hatfield during which time it worked a few railtours. In 1965 it was transferred to the Keighley & Worth Valley Railway where it remained until 1970 when it moved to Tyseley. Subsequently it spent some time at the North Yorkshire Moors Railway but is now based at the National Railway Museum.

GNR No. 1247 has had several homes on preserved lines since restoration, but outings on the main line have been few. However, on 16th September 1961 it headed the SBLC "Lea Flyer" special and is seen leaving Welwyn for Hertingfordbury and Hertford North.

J. G. Dewing

On 14th April 1962 No. 1247 took over an SLS special from Birmingham at Hatfield (above) and hauled it to Luton. A photographic stop was made at Ayot on the branch, as seen below.

Gavin Morrison

On 3rd July 1984 a private charter was organised by the Butterley Brick Company, and it is seen after arrival at Huddersfield behind No. 46229 *Duchess of Hamilton*.

John Whiteley

Either by chance or otherwise, No. 46229 *Duchess of Hamilton* makes a spectacular exit from Melling Tunnel at Wennington on 12th April 1982 with a "Trans Pennine Pullman".

Gavin Morrison

The Caledonian and North British liveries show up well in this picture of No. 123 and No. 256 *Glen Douglas* making a vigorous departure from Oban on 12th May 1962. The pair are returning to Glasgow via Callander with an SLS special.

Gavin Morrison

Shortly before sunset on 9th June 1984, No. 4498 *Sir Nigel Gresley* is crossing Milnsbridge Viaduct on the climb from Huddersfield to Standedge Tunnel with a return special from York to Manchester.

Gavin Morrison

A picture which by its **BR** appearance could have been taken in the 1960s, but was in fact taken on 8th September 1973 showing No. 60009 *Union of South Africa* near Wormit, having just crossed the Tay Bridge on its way back to Edinburgh. *Gavin Morrison*

The Garter Blue livery of No. 4468 *Mallard* contrasts sharply with the maroon stock of this special returning from Carnforth. The train is near Kettlesbeck Bridge on the beautiful afternoon of 16th May 1987 with Ingleborough clearly visible in the background. *John Whiteley*

To increase water capacity No. 4472 *Flying Scotsman* ran with two tenders for a spell in the 1960s. On 16th April 1967 it is leaving Leeds near Wortley South Junction with "The Mercian" railtour which provided a fitting main line steam finale for Leeds Central station.

Gavin Morrison

Flying Scotsman is seen again, this time coupled inside No. 1306 *Mayflower* near Thirsk on 21st September 1975. The pair are heading "The North Eastern" on its journey from Sheffield to Newcastle, No. 4771 *Green Arrow* having provided the motive power from Sheffield to York.

John Whiteley

No. 4771 *Green Arrow* both looked and sounded superb on 26th April 1986 as it roared past Midge Hill on the climb towards Diggle en route to York via Leeds.

John Whiteley

On 13th April 1964 No. 3442 *The Great Marquess* hauled a special from Leeds to Whitby for invited guests of the late Viscount Garnock. On the return journey it is leaving Goathland, on what is now the North Yorkshire Moors Railway, a scene which is now so familiar to the visitors of this popular preserved railway.

Gavin Morrison

With a full head of steam, No. 49 *Gordon Highlander* pauses at Carstairs on 16th October 1965 whilst working a special from Lanark to the Edinburgh area.

Gavin Morrison

No. 256 *Glen Douglas* is piloting Class J37 0-6-0 No. 64632 on 1st June 1963 as they climb from Bridge of Orchy near Achallader with the SLS "Jacobite" railtour to Fort William and Mallaig.

Gavin Morrison

On 7th September 1980 No. 246 *Morayshire* climbs steadily from Inverkeithing towards the Forth Bridge with "The Taysider" railtour from Falkirk to Dundee and back.

John Whiteley

No. 673 *Maude* glints in the early morning sun on 17th May 1980 shortly after leaving Kilmarnock, having been stabled there overnight on its epic journey from Falkirk to Rainhill.

John Whiteley

February 26th 1983 saw the outing of two smaller locomotives from the Severn Valley Railway stable. Nos 80079 and 43106 are near Lower Bullingham, shortly after leaving Hereford, with a "Welsh Marches Pullman" to Newport.
Gavin Morrison

Between heavy showers No. 92220 *Evening Star* catches a welcome patch of sunlight on its first main line outing since preservation. It is near Kettlesbeck Bridge on its way back to York from Carnforth on 31st May 1975.
Gavin Morrison

No. 990 *Henry Oakley*

Shortly after Ivatt had taken over responsibility of locomotive design for the Great Northern Railway he was faced with the need to provide more powerful express passenger locomotives to handle the increasing loads and heavier rolling stock, which was beyond the capability of the Stirling singles. He realised that the need was not for larger wheels and faster running, but greater pulling power which necessitated greater boiler power. Although he had already designed some inside-cylinder 4-4-0s for express passenger work, they were too short to carry a large enough boiler so the solution was to extend the frame and incorporate an extra carrying axle which in turn would accommodate a larger boiler. Thus the 4-4-2 Atlantic wheel arrangement came into being and in February 1897 Ivatt received permission to build an experimental passenger locomotive of this type. In May 1898 No. 990 appeared from Doncaster Works, the first British Atlantic tender engine. The GNR classification was C1 for all the Atlantics, but this was altered by the LNER to C2 for these original Atlantics, or "Klondykes" as they were nicknamed, and C1 was used for later, large Atlantics.

No. 990 was named *Henry Oakley* in June 1900 after a former General Manager of th GNR. Ten more of these "Klondykes" were built in 1900, one four-cylinder version in 1902 which was rebuilt in 1911 with two inside-cylinders, and a final batch of ten came out in 1903, making a total of 22 of these two-cylinder Atlantics with driving wheels of 6ft 8in diameter. They were all superheated from 1909 and several were fitted with new cylinders with piston valves, but by 1913 when all the large Atlantics were in service, they were relegated to secondary passenger duties. Withdrawal did not commence until 1935 and No. 3990 *Henry Oakley* was withdrawn from Lincoln in October 1937. It covered almost $1^1/4$ million miles in service and was restored to GNR livery after withdrawal and placed in York Museum in January 1938. It was restored to running order in 1953 and worked some special trains in connection with the centenary of Doncaster Works before eventually arriving at the National Railway Museum at York for exhibition purposes. For a brief period during the summer of 1977 it was loaned to the Keighley & Worth Valley Railway for use on their passenger trains but is now a prime static exhibit at York.

Even back in 1953 preserved steam locomotives were already attracting large crowds. The two Atlantics, with No. 990 *Henry Oakley* leading, are ready to leave the smokey atmosphere of King's Cross on the 'down' "Plant Centenarian" to Doncaster.

C. R. L. Coles

There cannot have been many finer sights in railway preservation than a couple of Great Northern Atlantics together on the main line. *Henry Oakley* pilots large-boilered No. 251 away from Grantham after a stop on 27th September 1953 on the 'up' "Plant Centenarian".

J. P. Wilson

A superb picture of the two famous Great Northern Atlantics, Nos 251 and 990 working in perfect harmony, both safety valves just blowing off and a slight exhaust from the chimney tops, as they pass Honington Junction on 27th September 1953 with the 'down' "Plant Centenarian". The train, from King's Cross to Doncaster, travelled via Lincoln on the outward trip.

J. P. Wilson

No. 251

Following the introduction of his original Atlantics, Ivatt designed a new series of Atlantics, the first of which, No. 251 appeared from Doncaster in December 1902. Even in comparison to the original Atlantics, No. 251 must have seemed enormous with its very much larger boiler and wide firebox, regarded by many as one of the most handsome engines ever to run in this country. It was monitored carefully for some time, but quantity production commenced in 1904 and eventually a total of 94 were built with the last one appearing in November 1910.

As soon as these large-boilered Atlantics appeared they were put to work on all the principal GNR expresses and all the main sheds had an allocation, each top-link crew having a regular engine kept in pristine condition. Until the Grouping all the C1s were allocated at King's Cross, New England, Grantham and Doncaster, but in later years a few were transferred to Copley Hill, Sheffield and York which was the furthest north they were allocated. They were used extensively on some of the Pullman trains putting up some remarkable performances until the appearanace of the pre-war streamlined trains which heralded the eclipse of Ivatt's large-boilered Atlantics which had given 30 years of distinguished service.

Initially the C1s appeared in standard GNR green livery, in which No. 251 is now preserved, but after the Grouping they were all gradually painted in standard LNER green livery, having had 3000 added to their numbers as part of the LNER renumbering scheme. This was altered again in January 1946 with the implementation of the 1943 renumbering scheme which allocated numbers commencing 2800 for the C1s. Withdrawal of the C1s commenced in 1943 and was accelerated after the war with the appearance of Thompson's B1 class 4-6-0s. Seventeen survived at Nationalisation, but only two were renumbered in the British Railways 628xx series, the last one, No. 62822 being withdrawn in November 1950. The pioneer, No. 251 was withdrawn in July 1947 as LNER No. 2800 and was then restored externally to GNR condition as part of the National Collection and like the earlier No. 990 *Henry Oakley* can now also be seen at the National Railway Museum at York.

A powerful picture of No. 251 piloting ex-GCR 'Director' class 4-4-0 No. 62663 *Prince Albert* on the "Farnborough Flyer" on 12th September 1954 near Arkwright Street, Nottingham.

J. P. Wilson

Another view of this famous special with Nos 251 and 62663, which originated at Leeds. The train was organised by No. 18 Group Royal Observer Corps to the Farnborough Air Show in Hampshire. Here, it is leading into the West Curve avoiding line round to Oxford Road box at Reading West station.

M. Earley courtesy C. R. L. Coles Collection

Shortly before closure of the branch No. 256 *Glen Douglas* visited Langholme on 6th April 1963, together with other lines in the Carlisle area.

Gavin Morrison

No. 256 *Glen Douglas* (62469)

Another one of the few surviving North British Railway locomotives is No. 256 *Glen Douglas* which has now been retired as a static exhibit to the Glasgow Museum of Transport. It was designed by William Paton Reid who succeeded Holmes as Locomotive Superintendent of the NBR in 1903. Reid was under pressure from the time he took up office to produce larger and more powerful engines for the NBR and one of several 4-4-0s which he produced was his Class K, of which 32 were built at Cowlairs between 1913 and 1920, including No. 256 *Glen Douglas* which was completed in September 1913. These 4-4-0s had slightly smaller coupled wheels of 6ft than some of his earlier 4-4-0s, and were designed specifically for working over the difficult West Highland line, hence the fact that all the locomotives were named after Glens, most of which were near the line over which they worked.

All 32 'Glens' were in service at the Grouping when they were reclassified D34 by the LNER. Throughout LNER days the majority of the 'Glens' were allocated to

Eastfield, several sub-shedded at Fort William and Mallaig for West Highland use. However, they also worked expresses between Glasgow and Edinburgh and Glasgow to Thornton and Dundee, and several 'Glens' were allocated to Thornton and St Margarets, those at the latter often working to Berwick, Hawick and Perth. All but two survived Nationalisation, but after the introduction of the B1 class 4-6-0s they became much more scattered and were reduced to more secondary work, several being transferred to the Great North of Scotland Section in 1953 to replace some of the older 4-4-0s which were then withdrawn.

The majority of 'Glens' were withdrawn from 1959, the last one surviving until November 1961. As BR No. 62469 *Glen Douglas* was withdrawn from traffic in 1959 and was restored to NBR livery at Cowlairs Works for working special trains in connection with the Scottish Industries Fair of that year. For several years it ran a variety of specials, but was finally retired in 1965, having been officially withdrawn in December 1962.

Most thought that 1st June 1963 would be the last day that steam would be seen on the famous West Highland line. On a glorious day *Glen Douglas* piloted ex-North British Railway J37 class No. 64632 and they are seen entering Arrochar & Tarbert. Unfortunately the J37 ran hot near Rannoch, and *Glen Douglas* dropped some fire bars and had to be helped into Fort William by Type 2 diesel electric No. D6137. After trouble with one of the two J37s that took the tour onto Mallaig, steam was abandoned and the train returned several hours late behind Type 2 diesel electric No. D5351.

Gavin Morrison

On 9th July 1981 *Glen Douglas* was working in the Border Counties on an RCTS special from Yorkshire. Piloting J37 class No. 64624, No. 256 is about to leave Greenlaw with the special to return to the Waverley Route at Ravenswood Junction.

Gavin Morrison

No. 49 *Gordon Highlander* (62277)

The Great North of Scotland Railway had only 334 route miles and 122 locomotives at the Grouping, and its last Locomotive Superintendent was Thomas Edward Heywood who was in office from 1914 until 1923.

Heywood introduced the superheated Class F 4-4-0 for the GNSR in 1920 and a total of eight were built during 1920 and 1921, being a development of Pickersgill's earlier saturated Class V 4-4-0. The Class F was the final 4-4-0 to be built by the GNSR with the result that they were used on the most important express passenger trains on the system until the early 1930s, by which time they had been reclassified D40 by the LNER in common with the Class V.

No. 49 *Gordon Highlander* was built by the North British Locomotive Co. in October 1920 and subsequently renumbered 6849 and later 2277 by the LNER, and finally 62277 by BR in November 1948. In common with the other D40s, it worked mainly between Aberdeen, Keith and Elgin initially, with the majority of the class of 21 allocated to Kittybrewster. However, after Nationalisation they tended to be relegated more to branch line work and were a regular sight between Craighellachie and Boat of Garten.

Withdrawal of the D40s was spread between 1946 and 1958 and *Gordon Highlander* was the last to be withdrawn, in June 1958 having latterly been a regular performer on the Speyside line. On withdrawal it was restored to GNSR green livery at Inverurie Works as No. 49, not strictly correct as this engine had only run in black livery on the GNSR, as introduced by Heywood. In restored condition it worked normal services on the Speyside line for a short period before being transferred to Dawsholm shed where it joined the other Scottish preserved engines for periodic use on specials before being retired to the Glasgow Museum of Transport as a static exhibit.

On 18th September 1959 No. 49 *Gordon Highlander* is coupled inside Caledonian No. 123 heading a special train in connection with the Scottish Industries Fair. The pair are arriving at Glasgow Kelvin Hall.

J. G. Dewing

The steep bank near Loanhead proved just a little too much for No. 49 on 16th October 1965, and it stalled very conveniently just in front of the photographer.

Gavin Morrison

No. 4472 *Flying Scotsman* (60103)

Herbert Nigel Gresley was appointed Locomotive Superintendent of the Great Northern Railway in October 1911, succeeding H. A. Ivatt, and assumed the post of Chief Mechanical Engineer of the newly formed LNER in 1923. He was to hold that post for 18 years until he died in office on 5th April 1941 and had been awarded a knighthood in the King's Birthday Honours of 1936. After the Grouping he reorganised the locomotive works and concentrated new construction principally at Doncaster and Darlington continuing the "big engine" policy of the LNER.

Following the First World War, which had generated particularly heavy passenger train loads, which were often beyond the limits of the large-boiled Ivatt Atlantics, Gresley was aware of the need for larger, more powerful engines. He introduced his large-boiled K3 class 2-6-0 in 1920 and the success of this design convinced him that a six-coupled engine was essential for future main line passenger power. Designs were therefore prepared for a large taper-boiled three-cylinder Pacific and in April 1922 No.1470 *Great Northern* appeared from Doncaster – the first of his GNR Class A1 Pacifics. It was soon followed by a second and the GNR then ordered a further ten which were also built at Doncaster and delivered after the Grouping, including No. 1472 which was delivered in February 1923. It was renumbered 4472 and named *Flying Scotsman* in February 1924 in readiness for the 1924 Empire Exhibition at Wembley and was destined to become one of the most famous locomotives of all time. A further 40 A1 Pacifics were ordered, 20 were built at Doncaster during 1924 and 1925 and 20 were built by the North British Locomotive Co. in 1924. In 1927 Gresley decided to replace the original 180lb boilers with 220lb boilers and incorporate long-travel valve gear. All the A1s were rebuilt in this way by 1948 and reclassified A3 (except *Great Northern* which was rebuilt in a different manner by Edward Thompson) and a further 27 Pacifics were built at Doncaster between 1928 and 1935 to the new A3 class design.

Near Raskelf north of York on the East Coast Main Line No. 4472 is heading north to Newcastle on 28th September 1975.

John Whiteley

On one of its many outings over the Settle and Carlisle line No. 4472 *Flying Scotsman* struggles towards Ais Gill Summit on 30th January 1983 when it was working a special for the AGM of SLOA. Note that the tender from A4 class No. 4498 *Sir Nigel Gresley* was attached to the locomotive at this period.

John Whiteley

On 1st May 1928 No. 4472 *Flying Scotsman* was again in the limelight when it hauled the first non-stop London-Edinburgh express, made possible by Gresley's design of a corridor tender which enabled a crew change mid journey. Although the A3s continued to be the mainstay of East Coast Main Line express passenger traffic, they lost their corridor tenders to the streamlined A4 Pacifics which took over the non-stop workings. No more major changes were made to the A3s until BR rebuilt them with Kylchap double blastpipe and chimneys from 1957, following experiments almost 20 years earlier with one of the A3s, No. 2751 *Humorist*. The results were remarkable and it succeeded in giving the A3s a new lease of life.

In their latter days most of the A3s were fitted with German style trough type smoke deflectors, *Flying Scotsman* being dealt with in December 1961, having been fitted with a double chimney in January 1959. It was withdrawn in January 1963 and purchased by Mr Alan Pegler for restoration to working order in LNER lined green passenger livery with single chimney. After hauling a variety of specials in this country it visited the United States late in 1970 and was rescued from there in February 1973 when it was purchased by Mr W. H. McAlpine. It is now owned by Flying Scotsman Enterprises Ltd and based at Steamtown, Carnforth, but went to Australia for 1988-89 for inclusion in the Bicentenary celebrations.

The last time steam climbed Shap from the south was on 29th June 1969. *Flying Scotsman* is seen on this occasion passing Greenholme in fine style. It was attached to two tenders for several trips during this period.

John Whiteley

Flying Scotsman approaches Doncaster at Bridge Junction on the 'down' slow line on 6th March 1983.

John Whiteley

On one of its rare visits to the Calder Valley line No. 4472 passes through Ludendenfoot Cutting on 1st June 1969.

Gavin Morrison

Vast crowds witnessed *Flying Scotsman's* impressive departure from Peterborough for York on 6th March 1983.
John Whiteley

The second commemorative train in memory of Bishop Eric Treacy ran over the Settle and Carlisle line on 30th September 1978. The sun came out as *Flying Scotsman* crossed Ribblehead Viaduct as it headed north.

John Whiteley

Flying Scotsman has now been running around for 25 years since preservation, and in the early years it was used to work a Gainsborough Model Railway Society special to Weymouth on 12th September 1965. It is seen passing Polkesdown on the outskirts of Bournemouth.

Gavin Morrison

No. 246 *Morayshire* (62712)

Gresley's first passenger engine design for the LNER after its formation in 1923 was a three-cylinder 4-4-0 which was classified D49. They were built for intermediate passenger duties to replace some of the ageing pre-Grouping 4-4-0s, and when they first entered service were the largest 4-4-0s of the "Big Four". In all, 76 D49s were built at Darlington between 1927 and 1935, No. 246 *Morayshire* appearing in February 1928.

Morayshire was one of 34 D49/1s which had Walschaerts valve gear with piston valves, the D49/2s having rotary cam poppet valve gear. All the D49s were given the names of Counties (mostly Shires) or Hunts, and eventually all the Counties (or Shires) were Class D49/1 and the Hunts were Class D49/2.

The D49/2s were generally associated with work in Scotland and the North East of England and of the first batch of 20 engines, 6 were allocated to Neville Hill, Leeds, the other 14 engines (including *Morayshire*) being given the names of Scottish Counties and being allocated to Scottish area sheds. Full LNER apple green passenger livery was given to the D49s when introduced, and *Morayshire* is faithfully restored in this livery, although its original 4,200 gallon "Group Standard" tender was replaced by an ex-GCR tender in 1941 which has been rebuilt since preservation.

The D49s were at their peak working intermediate passenger services in the pre-war period, but after the war many of their former duties were handed over to Thompson's mixed traffic Class B1 4-6-0s and withdrawals commenced in 1957. *Morayshire* had been shedded at Dundee, Perth, Haymarket, St Margarets, Thornton Junction and finally Hawick when withdrawn from service as BR No. 62712 in July 1961 as the last surviving member of the class. Fortunately, instead of immediately being subjected to the cutter's torch. *Morayshire* was moved to Slateford laundry, Edinburgh, for use as a stationary boiler until January 1962. Shortly afterwards Mr Ian Fraser secured her purchase and following initial restoration at Inverurie Works it was eventually handed over to the Royal Scottish Museum in Edinburgh and subsequently loaned to the Scottish Railway Preservation Society at Falkirk for return to main line running.

No. 246 *Morayshire's* activities since preservation have all been north of the border, except when it came south in 1975 for the Stockton & Darlington 150th celebrations. On 5th July 1981 it was photographed climbing from Inverkeithing to North Queensferry.

John Whiteley

Working from Dundee to Falkirk on 19th April 1981 *Morayshire* is near Cowdenbeath at Lumphinans.

John Whiteley

Having completed its first public outing after restoration, *Morayshire* hauls the empty carriage stock near Larbert as the sun sets on 7th September 1980.

John Whiteley

Another view of the tour on 7th September 1980 as No. 246 heads north for Dundee near Wormit.

John Whiteley

On 19th April 1981 No. 246 is seen heading north to Dundee and crossing Markinch Viaduct.

Gavin Morrison

No. 60009 *Union of South Africa*

Despite his extremely successful A1 (later A3) class Pacifics, Gresley will always be remembered for his streamlined three-cylinder A4 class Pacifics. They were designed specifically for working relatively light trains at high speed. Initially this was the "Silver Jubilee" streamlined train which was introduced in the autumn of 1935 between London and Newcastle. In March 1935 four A4s were ordered from Doncaster Works and No. 2509 *Silver Link* was the first one to be completed in September of that same year, top priority having been given to its construction.

On 27th September, three days before the regular train went into service, *Silver Link* made a trial publicity run with the new "Silver Jubilee' stock from King's Cross to Grantham which proved to be the most remarkable debut ever made by a steam locomotive. During the journey speed touched 112^1/2mph on two occasions and people thronging the lineside must have been impressed by the magnificent spectacle of both engine and train finished in striking silver-grey livery racing through the countryside. The other three A4s were completed before the end of 1935, and in 1936 another 31 were ordered from Doncaster, all of which were in service by the summer of 1938.

A powerful picture of No. 60009 breasting the sharp rise out of Dundee at Dock Street Tunnel on 14th April 1979, whilst heading for Aberdeen from Edinburgh.

John Whiteley

No. 4488 *Union of South Africa* was completed in June 1937 and was one of five A4s selected for use on a second streamlined train, the "Coronation", and specially painted in a matching garter blue livery which was later adopted as standard for the whole class. *Union of South Africa* was paired with a corridor tender which had been built in 1928 for a non-streamlined Pacific and was allocated to Haymarket where it remained until May 1962 when it was moved to Aberdeen Ferryhill from where it was withdrawn in June 1966.

Between May 1957 and November 1958 double blastpipes and chimneys were fitted to all the A4s not so fitted from new, and as BR No. 60009 *Union of South Africa* was dealt with in November 1958, by then in the standard BR green livery with orange and black lining in which condition it is now preserved. On withdrawal it was acquired by a group of four businessmen headed by Mr John Cameron who formed the Lochty Private Railway Company based near Anstruther in East Fife.

No. 60009 *Union of South Africa's* visit south of the border for several trips in 1984 was very popular with enthusiasts. On 9th August 1984 it was working the "Scarborough Spa Express", and it is seen here being prepared to leave Platform 9 at York for the east coast.

John Whiteley

Only very rarely has there been the opportunity to photograph No. 60009 heading south out of Edinburgh whilst in preservation. On 27th April 1985 it was working round the suburban line and is leaving Calton Tunnel, shortly after leaving Waverley station.   *Gavin Morrison*

No. 60009 heads south from Aberdeen for Edinburgh under one of the famous signal gantries on 1st September 1979.   *John Whiteley*

No. 4498 *Sir Nigel Gresley* (60007)

No. 4498 was completed in November 1937, was the one hundredth Gresley Pacific to be built and was named *Sir Nigel Gresley* after its designer. It appeared in garter blue livery and was also coupled to a corridor tender which had been built in 1928 and which had been taken from a non-streamlined Pacific. It was initially allocated to King's Cross and was soon hard at work on the East Coast Main Line participating in some of the non-stop running. In common with other A4s after Nationalisation, No. 60007 *Sir Nigel Gresley* was provided with a double chimney, in December 1957, and when King's Cross "Top Shed" was closed in June 1963 it was one of

eleven A4s still in service there which were transferred to New England. When the remaining A4s were finally displaced from the Eastern Region by new diesels *Sir Nigel Gresley* was transferred to the Scottish Region and enjoyed a final fling working from Aberdeen Ferryhill on the former Caledonian main line between Aberdeen and Glasgow. After withdrawal in February 1966 *Sir Nigel Gresley* was taken to Crewe Works by its new owners, the A4 Locomotive Society Ltd and restored to perfect working condition in garter blue livery as No. 4498, but still having a double chimney which of course it never had in LNER days.

The cold and winter sunshine produce a superb exhaust as No. 4498 *Sir Nigel Gresley* climbs Hatton Bank on a Marylebone-Sheffield special on 6th February 1988, with *Ethel 3* behind the engine for train heating.

John Whiteley

On 22nd September 1984 No. 4498 leaves Hull for Scarborough.

Gavin Morrison

On its only visit to Aberdeen since preservation *Sir Nigel Gresley* storms out of the "Granite City" past Ferryhill back to Edinburgh on 22nd June 1974.

John Whiteley

No. 60019 *Bittern*

No. 4464 *Bittern* was completed in December 1937 and turned out in garter blue livery but coupled to a streamlined non-corridor tender. It was one of seven A4s (all Newcastle based engines) which was never coupled to a corridor tender. Initially *Bittern* was allocated to Heaton, but was transferred to Gateshead in March 1943 where it remained until the end of 1963 when it too was transferred to Scotland and participated in working the three hour Glasgow expresses from Aberdeen whilst allocated to Ferryhill. No. 60019

Bittern was one of the last two A4s to remain in service, and they were both withdrawn in September 1966. Soon after withdrawal it was purchased by Mr G. S. Drury of York and was housed in York North shed from where it worked some enthusiasts' specials until the BR ban on steam hauled trains was imposed in November 1967. It was then stored at Neville Hill, Leeds and Walton Colliery, before being transferred to Dinting, still with its original tender.

No. 60019 *Bittern* crosses the River Eden at Carlisle en route from Leeds to Glasgow on 16th July 1967.

Gavin Morrison

On 21st April 1973 the line between Scarborough and Hull saw steam in the shape of No. 19 *Bittern* near Speeton after one track had been taken out of use prior to the line being singled. On 17th June 1973 it is heading for Scarborough from York near Kirkham Priory.

Both P.J. Fitton

Near Crawford on the West Coast Main Line on 16th July 1967. During 1988 *Bittern* was repainted in LNER grey livery and took on the guise of No. 2509 *Silver Link*. It would be nice to think that it may subsequently be restored to running order in this condition as sadly, none of the original A4s which were turned out in this eye-catching livery have survived.

John Whiteley

No. 4468 *Mallard* (60022)

During construction of the A4s drawings appeared for a double blastpipe and chimney which was fitted to No. 4468 *Mallard* which was completed in March 1938. It was one of four A4s which were fitted with this arrangement when built and these proved to be particularly free steaming engines.

Mallard had spells at Doncaster, Grantham and King's Cross and secured immortality on 3rd July 1938 when it established the steam locomotive speed record of 126mph, whilst working high speed brake tests between London and Peterborough with a premeditated fast run on the return from Stoke Tunnel to Peterborough. Having concluded the brake trials the train, which comprised the dynamometer car and three of the "Coronation" twin-coach sets, proceeded to Barkston where it turned and was briefly prepared. After Grantham the acceleration up to Stoke Tunnel was phenomenal and within minutes the record had been secured for all time.

When *Mallard* was withdrawn from King's Cross in April 1963 it went to Doncaster for restoration to virtually its original condition, including the side skirting both behind and in front of the cylinders which had been removed from all the A4s during the war. It was then hauled to Nine Elms Yard in London and moved by road into the British Transport Museum at Clapham, where it stayed until being moved to the newly established National Railway Museum at York as a static exhibit in the Main Hall. In 1985 it was restored to main line running condition and appears periodically on the main line as part of the National Collection.

Mallard passes Kilnhurst near Rotherham on 8th November 1986.

John Whiteley

Below and Right: No. 4468 *Mallard* leaves York for Harrogate on 26th April 1987. *John Whiteley*

Right: No. 4468 is seen from the Humber Bridge as it passes Ferriby, on 8th July 1986.
Gavin Morrison

The return of No. 4468 *Mallard* to main line running after 23 years was the highlight of the steam preservation scene in 1986. Working a special from Marylebone to York on 8th November 1986, it is seen passing Duffield.
John Whiteley

No. 4771 *Green Arrow* (60800)

In response to a need for a heavy mixed-traffic engine to work a new LNER fast goods service in the mid-1930s, Gresley designed a three-cylinder 2-6-2 which emerged from Doncaster in June 1936. No. 4771 *Green Arrow*, was the first of what was to become a total of 184 engines of Class V2.

Initially only five were built at Doncaster, but after evaluating the design, further construction commenced at both Doncaster and Darlington, the last engine entering service in 1944 after construction of these extremely useful engines had continued throughout the war.

Because of their weight and heavy axle-loading they were restricted to the same route availability as the Pacifics, but because of their relatively large coupled wheel diameter of 6ft 2in they were also suitable for express passenger duties. Whilst the V2s did most of their work on the East Coast Main Line, they were also to be seen on the Great Central Main Line and in Scotland, and will forever be associated with the now closed Waverley route.

No. 4771 *Green Arrow* was turned out in full LNER apple green livery, in which it is now preserved. In early BR days the class was painted in black lined-out mixed-traffic livery, but in their final years they were given Brunswick green livery with orange and black lining. Withdrawal of the V2s commenced early in 1962 and the last V2 to be withdrawn from service was No. 60836 in December 1966. As BR No. 60800 *Green Arrow* was withdrawn in August 1962 when allocated to King's Cross. It was restored to LNER apple green livery at Doncaster Works, after which it was stored at various locations and finally put into main line running order as part of the National Collection, the sole survivor of the class.

The fireman on No. 4771 *Green Arrow* leans out to observe his efforts with the shovel as it leaves Sheffield for a trip up the Hope Valley on 21st April 1979. The location is alongside the British Rail Social Club, and no doubt the exhaust caused some comment in the club later in the day. *Gavin Morrison*

Green Arrow passes Goose Hill Junction, Normanton on a special from Sheffield to Newcastle on 21st September 1975. This once important junction has now been removed, with closure of the old Midland Main Line as a through route to Sheffield.   *John Whiteley*

The exhaust positions itself perfectly for this picture of *Green Arrow* storming out of Marsh Lane Cutting, Leeds with a test train from York via Harrogate on 15th March 1978.
                                                    John Whiteley

No. 4771 bursts out of Wescoe Hill Tunnel on the Leeds to Harrogate line on 7th April 1979.

John Whiteley

No. 3442 *The Great Marquess* (61994)

The Great Marquess was one of six K4 class 2-6-0s designed by Sir Nigel Gresley specifically for use on the tough West Highland line when more powerful locomotives were required. Nos 3441–3446 were built at Darlington, entering traffic between January 1937 and January 1939. No. 3442 *The Great Marquess* entered traffic in July 1938, and for a short time was named *MacCailein Mór*.

Although the first one of these three-cylinder Moguls was turned out in black livery, the remaining five locomotives were given full LNER apple green passenger livery, which was subsequently given to No. 3441. These mixed-traffic engines had 5ft 2in driving wheels and were soon working well on the West Highland lines. However, when maintenance standards suffered during the war their performance deteriorated and they gained a reputation for poor riding characteristics.

In 1945 Edward Thompson rebuilt one of the K4s,

No. 3445, as a two-cylinder engine, becoming the prototype for the K1 class 2-6-0s. The remaining five K4s were relegated to secondary duties by the early 1950s, and in 1959 were all transferred to Thornton Junction shed where they stayed until withdrawal during 1961. As BR No. 61994 *The Great Marquess* was withdrawn in December 1961, but it was purchased by the late Viscount Garnock and restored to working order in LNER livery at Cowlairs Works. In April 1963 it worked a special goods train to Neville Hill, Leeds, where it stayed for over nine years during which time it worked a number of enthusiasts' specials. In September 1972 it was transferred to its new home on the Severn Valley Railway where further extensive restoration work is being carried out at the time of writing in anticipation of its re-appearance on the main line, which may remarkably include service on the West Highland once again.

The RCTS "Dalesman" tour was the first outing for No. 3442 *The Great Marquess* following preservation. After visiting the Otley and Ilkley line to Skipton, and the Grassington branch, the tour headed into Lancashire. The picture shows the tour passing Earby on 4th May 1963. The unfamiliarity of the Midland crews and the locomotive being badly 'off beat' contributed to a very late return back to Yorkshire.   *Gavin Morrison*

The Railway Correspondence and Travel Society organised a special with *The Great Marquess* up the Weardale branch as far as St John's Chapel on 10th April 1965. The train is seen passing the scenic little station of Westgate in Weardale.   *Gavin Morrison*

Another picture of *The Great Marquess* on its first outing after preservation. The train is passing Manningham station, Bradford on 4th May 1963.   *John Whiteley*

The last train over the Selby to Driffield line was this Stephenson Locomotive Society special headed by *The Great Marquess* piloting the now preserved K1 class No. 62005 on 6th March 1965. This tour was also the last train between Scarborough and Whitby, and the pair is seen taking the Driffield line at Market Weighton.   *Gavin Morrison*

No. 1306 *Mayflower* (61306)

When Sir Nigel Gresley (having been awarded a knighthood in 1936) died in office on 5th April 1941 he was succeeded as CME of the LNER by Edward Thompson. Thompson realised that simplicity of design and ease of maintenance were of paramount importance during the difficult wartime years, and whilst he will be best remembered for his designs of this nature, particularly his Class B1 4-6-0s, he will also be remembered for rebuilding a number of Gresley's revered express passenger engines in a rather tactless manner.

During these wartime years the LNER was short of a medium powered mixed-traffic engine with a wide route availability, as Gresley's excellent V2s were too heavy for many of the lines where mixed-traffic engines were needed. To meet this requirement drawings were prepared and the first batch of ten of Thompson's Class B1 4-6-0s were ordered from Darlington Works in August 1942, the first one appearing in December 1942. Construction of a further 400 B1s was announced by the LNER in 1945 as part of its five year modernisation programme, which included 30 that had previously been ordered in 1944 from Darlington. Construction of the B1s continued until 1952 when the last one was completed by the North British Locomotive Co.

No. 61306 was completed in April 1948 by the North British Locomotive Co. at their Queens Park Works, and appearing as it did after Nationalisation, never carried an LNER No. 1306, in which guise it is now preserved. During its BR days it was not named, the name *Mayflower* being carried by B1 No. 61379.

Although classed as a mixed-traffic locomotive, with their 6ft 2in coupled driving wheels it is fair to say that the B1s were more at home on passenger workings than on freights. Initially they were concentrated in East Anglia and on the Great Central Section, although two of the first ten B1s were sent to Scotland. However, by the early years of Nationalisation they were to be found all over the lines of the old LNER and eventually beyond, following regional boundary changes. No. 61306 was the last B1 to travel up the Great Central line to Marylebone in August 1966 before closure, and survived to be one of the last three B1s in active service, finally being withdrawn on 30th September 1967 after working the last steam hauled portion of the "Yorkshire Pullman" from Bradford Exchange to Leeds earlier that day. Following withdrawal it was purchased privately from BR and restored to working order at Carnforth in LNER livery and named *Mayflower*. Although enjoying a spell of main line duty in the 1970s, it is now in regular service on the Great Central Railway from its base at Loughborough.

Millom curve is a fine location to portray a double header. On 8th May 1976 No. 1306 *Mayflower* teamed up with *Flying Scotsman* for a trip up the Cumbrian Coast from Carnforth to Sellafield.

John Whiteley

Mayflower and *Green Arrow* are approaching Seascale, returning from Sellafield to Carnforth on 21st June 1975.

John Whiteley

Plenty of action as *Mayflower* leaves Carnforth for Sellafield on 8th April 1978. This was one of the few occasions that the locomotive worked by itself on the main line.

Gavin Morrison

York is the destination of the special headed by *Mayflower* as it leaves Carnforth on 12th June 1977, another occasion when it worked on its own.   *John Whiteley*

This 14 coach train presents no problems for *Mayflower* and *Flying Scotsman* as they pass the summit of Lindal Bank en route to Carnforth on 8th May 1976.   *Gavin Morrison*

No. 2005 (62005)

In 1945 drawings were prepared for rebuilding Gresley three-cylinder class K4 2-6-0 No. 3445 *MacCailin Mor* to Thompson's standard two-cylinder arrangement with a shortened version of his B1 boiler. This rebuilding was completed at Doncaster in December 1945 and the prototype was initially classified K1, but was reclassified K1/1 to make way for the production engines, a total of 70 of which were ordered in July 1947 from the North British Locomotive Co. Thompson had retired before the first of the K1s were completed and some minor modifications were made to the design by his successor, A. H. Peppercorn who was appointed CME in June 1946.

All the K1s appeared during 1949 and 1950, No. 62005 appearing in June 1949 in the standard fully lined out BR black livery, initially with the lettering "British Railways" on the tender, and not the lion and wheel emblem. The two-cylinder class K1 2-6-0s had 5ft 2in diameter coupled wheels and proved to be almost as versatile as Thompson's B1 class 4-6-0s and were all initially allocated to the Eastern Region and North Eastern Region. However, in 1952 five K1s were transferred from March to Scotland for use on West Highland trains to replace the ageing K2s, and stayed there until 1961. No. 62005 spent all its life in the North East being shedded at Heaton, Darlington, Ardsley, York, North Blyth and Holbeck, Leeds. Although officially withdrawn on 30th December 1967 as the last of its class and the last steam engine on the Eastern Region, No. 62005 was subsequently towed to Port Clarence where it acted as stationary boiler for the works for almost six weeks, after which it was returned to Leeds Neville Hill shed where it was stored for several years.

Viscount Garnock, who had already secured the purchase of *The Great Marquess,* had obtained an option on No. 62005 with a view to exchanging boilers, but when this seemed unnecessary it left No. 62005 available for preservation. A consortium of four eventually purchased the locomotive and promptly donated it to the North Eastern Locomotive Preservation Group in 1972 for restoration as No. 2005 in LNER apple green livery, at the request of the former owners, but which livery it of course had never carried previously. The restoration work was successfully completed at Thornaby in May 1974 after two years of painstaking work by dedicated enthusiasts. Apart from working regularly on the North Yorkshire Moors Railway it has proved to be a very reliable engine on a variety of main line outings, including a considerable amount of work between Fort William and Mallaig.

Whitby harbour and the abbey make a splendid background to this picture of No. 2005 leaving on a special which it was working to Battersby on 28th March 1979.
John Whiteley

On 13th June 1987 No. 2005 is near Cemetery North Junction, shortly after leaving West Hartlepool, with an early morning departure from Middlesbrough at the start of its journey to Fort William, for its summer season.
J.R.P. Hunt

The owners of No. 2005, the North Eastern Locomotive Preservation Group (NELPG), organised this Pullman special over the Settle and Carlisle on 20th March 1983. No. 2005 is approaching Settle, just beyond the bottom of the long climb to Blea Moor from Settle Junction. *John Whiteley*

No. 2005 worked the second steam passenger train over the Fort William to Glasgow section of the West Highland line since 1963, the first being worked by No. 5305 (see page 99). It is seen making a vigorous start from Bridge of Orchy on 14th November 1987. *J.R.P. Hunt*

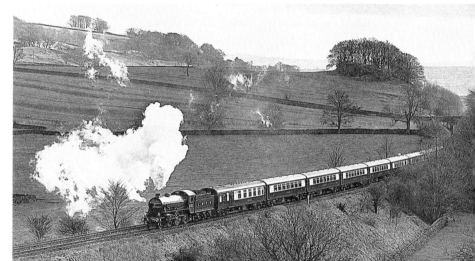

The superb scenery of the West Highland Mallaig extension is shown in this picture of No. 2005 drifting round the curve at the head of Loch Eilt on 27th September 1987.

J.R.P. Hunt

At the head of Loch Sheil is the famous concrete Glenfinnan Viaduct. The length is 416 yards on 21 spans, each of which is 50 feet wide, and it is built on a sharp curve. Spectacular views are available from all sides, but this fine picture of No. 2005 is taken from the south side of the Mallaig end. The Fort William-Mallaig line offers what is probably the finest scenery available on any line in the country. This picture was taken on 17th September 1987.

J.R.P. Hunt

BR Standards

No. 75069

The three designs of H. G. Ivatt for the LMS immediately before Nationalisation paved the way for the standard designs of British Railways. This final stage in British steam locomotive design was put in the hands of Robert A. Riddles who was appointed Member of the Railway Executive for Mechanical and Electrical Engineering. He had a team of mainly ex-LMS men who helped to co-ordinate work from the various drawing offices which were involved in producing the BR standard designs. The best aspects from the practices of the previous "Big Four" companies were incorporated in the new designs, but the emphasis was very much on ease of maintenance and simplicity of operation.

In all, twelve standard classes were produced by BR and a total of 999 locomotives were built before the end of the steam era on British Railways. The use of two cylinders was decided upon for all new standard locomotives and the first standard BR locomotive made its debut in January 1951 in the shape of No. 70000 *Britannia,* which has been preserved, but has not yet seen main line service. Later in 1951, in May, the first of 80 lightweight Class 4 4-6-0 mixed-traffic locomotives appeared. They were all built at Swindon and No. 75069

emerged in September 1955 and was destined to have a working life on BR of only eleven years. They were amongst the most popular of the standard classes and their low axle loading of 17tons 5cwt gave them an excellent route availability.

When new No. 75069 was one of 15 which were allocated to the Southern Region, No. 75069 going to Dover. Following draughting tests at Swindon, several standard Class 4 4-6-0s were given double blastpipes and chimneys from 1957 onwards, including No. 75069. This was also one of 30 which were fitted with the large flush sided tender. Although further standard Class 4 4-6-0s were ordered for the Eastern Region, these were cancelled as dieselisation progressed, which was ultimately responsible for the withdrawal of the standard classes which were far from life expired. No. 75069 was withdrawn from Eastleigh in September 1966 and ended up in the Barry scrapyard before being rescued and restored to working order at the Severn Valley Railway. Since then it has seen regular service on the Severn Valley Railway, as well as working a variety of main line excursions.

The participants on the "William Shakespeare" special from Marylebone to Stratford upon Avon appear to be having a good run behind No. 75069 as it storms past Gerrards Cross on 12th April 1986. *Pete Skelton*

"The Red Dragon" special had No. 75069 as its motive power from Newport to Swindon. The locomotive made an excellent climb up the 1 in 74 and 1 in 60 section near Frampton Mansell en route to Swindon on 2nd March 1985.

John Whiteley

The tide is out in the Dovey Estuary at Barmouth as No. 75069 crosses the bridge en route to Machynlleth on 28th May 1987.

L.A. Nixon

No. 75069 hurries along the level track between Newport and Severn Tunnel Junction past Magor with the "Red Dragon" special to Swindon on 2nd March 1985.

John Whiteley

No. 80079

Bearing in mind the BR standard classes had such short working lives, relatively few locomotives have been preserved and only a handful have seen main line service. However, no fewer than 15 of the excellent BR 2-6-4Ts have either been preserved or scheduled for preservation at the time of writing. Only one class of 2-6-4T was introduced by BR and it was based very closely on the LMS 2-6-4Ts introduced by Stanier, and later developed by Fairburn.

A total of 155 of these mixed-traffic locomotives were built at Derby, Brighton and Doncaster between 1951 and 1956. No. 80079 was built at Brighton and entered service in March 1954, being allocated initially to Plaistow and then to Tilbury where it remained for eight years and shared passenger workings in South Essex from Fenchurch Street. The BR 2-6-4Ts entered service on all Regions except the Western, although towards the end of the steam era several were transferred to the Western Region from the Tilbury line, including No. 80079, when these services were electrified. No. 80079 went to Croes Newydd, Wrexham and for its last few years of service worked over the Cambrian system, to Chester, and also on the Severn Valley line before closure, and where appropriately it is now preserved.

As suburban electrification and dieselisation progressed during the 1960s the BR 2-6-4Ts were steadily withdrawn, and No. 80079 was withdrawn from Croes Newydd in July 1965 and sold to Woodham's scrapyard at Barry after a mere eleven years of service. It was rescued from there in 1971 after funds had been raised by Severn Valley Railway members and entered service on the railway in 1977 after completion of a major overhaul.

Certainly one of the most lively performances put up on the Hereford to Newport line by preserved locomotives, was on 26th February 1983 when Severn Valley Railway locomotives Nos 80079 and 43106 hauled the "Welsh Marches Pullman". On the return the crew decided to see what No. 80079 could do virtually on its own as the train left Abergavenny up the 1 in 85 climb. The sound was incredible.   *Gavin Morrison*

Another view of Nos 80079 and 43106 heading north on the "Welsh Marches Pullman" near Ponthir on 26th February 1983.

John Whiteley

No. 80080

Another newcomer to the main line in 1988 was BR Standard 2-6-4T No. 80080 which is now based at the Midland Railway Centre, Butterley. Like sister locomotive No. 80079, also featured in this book, it was completed at Brighton Works in March 1954, and it too took up duties from Plaistow shed handling commuter services from Fenchurch Street to Barking, Tilbury, Southend and Shoeburyness. When the London, Tilbury and Southend lines were electrified in the summer of 1962, No. 80080 spent a brief period in store before it was transferred to Croes Newydd, Wrexham. Whilst there it was used very successfully on the former Cambrian lines from Oswestry to Machynlleth and along the coast to Pwllheli and Aberystwyth. With the arrival of diesel multiple units these mixed-traffic 2-6-4Ts became redundant and No. 80080 was withdrawn in July 1965 from Croes Newydd from where it went to Barry. In November 1980 it left Barry by road for Matlock, the base of the Peak Railway Society and has since been painstakingly restored to main line standards at Butterley. Its progress, from Barry rescue to completion of restoration was followed by the BBC television programme 'Blue Peter'.

Sporting a Plaistow shed plate, No. 80080 is seen stopping for water at Gloucester on the evening of 17th September 1988 on its journey from Butterley to Salisbury for working specials to Yeovil Junction and Romsey.

Pete Skelton

No. 92203 *Black Prince*

The 9F 2-10-0 heavy goods locomotive was the last of the BR standard designs to appear, and it was probably the most successful. Design work at Brighton did not commence until 1951 as a heavy freight engine was low on the building priority list. However, between 1954 and 1960 251 were built, 198 at Crewe and the remainder at Swindon. Initially a 2-8-2 wheel arrangement had been considered for this heavy freight engine, but in the event Riddles decided upon a 2-10-0 wheel arrangement with 5ft diameter coupled driving wheels.

Although very efficient, powerful freight engines, the 9Fs will probably be best remembered more as mixed-traffic engines. It was the Western Region which first used them regularly on Saturday extras to the West Country and occasionally on South Wales expresses from the late 1950s, and before long they were being used by both the London Midland Region and Eastern Region on passenger workings. In 1960, at the eleventh hour of the Somerset & Dorset, they were introduced and proved to be ideal engines for this difficult route, and did some excellent work on passenger turns during the summer timetable.

No. 92203 was built at Swindon in April 1959 and was one of 68 9Fs built with a double chimney, a few earlier engines being similarly fitted later. It was initially allocated to St Philip's Marsh, Bristol, and after less than ten years service, was withdrawn from Birkenhead in November 1967. It was purchased by the artist David Shepherd, named *Black Prince,* and is now based at Cranmore on the East Somerset Railway.

In connection with an open day at Eastleigh, on 13th May 1973 a series of specials were organised between Eastleigh and Romsey, and No. 92203 *Black Prince* is seen near Chandlers Ford.

R. Cover

On 19th May 1973 *Black Prince* worked a special to Worcester for the Wirral Railway Circle and it is seen here coasting leisurely along near Wyre Piddle on the single line section through the Cotswolds.

John Whiteley

No. 92220 *Evening Star*

No. 92220 *Evening Star* is possibly the most famous freight engine of all time. It was the last 9F to be built, the last steam locomotive to be built at Swindon and the final steam locomotive to be built for service on British Railways before the complete changeover to diesel and electric traction. Not surprisingly, it was immediately scheduled for preservation as soon as its active service for BR was finished, and in the event was the shortest-lived member of the class of 251 in service on BR.

No. 92220 was delivered from Swindon in March 1960 in full BR passenger green livery and had a GWR style copper cap to its double chimney, in true Swindon tradition. It was the only 9F to be named in BR days, and was given the name *Evening Star* at a special ceremony at Swindon on 18th March 1960, a special commemorative plaque being fitted beneath each nameplate. After delivery it was allocated to Cardiff Canton and was kept in excellent condition, occasionally deputising on express passenger duties, including the "Red Dragon", which at that period was diagrammed for a 'Britannia' Pacific. It was specially

transferred to Bath Motive Power Depot in August 1962 to work the last southbound "Pines Express" to run over the Somerset & Dorset line, which it did unassisted on Saturday 8th September 1962. It was a heavy twelve coach train which was handled with consummate ease, proving what excellent locomotives the 9Fs were and how ideally suited they were to the Somerset & Dorset line. Sadly they came too late to save the line and all long distance and through trains were diverted away after the end of the 1962 summer services. Surprisingly *Evening Star* re-appeared on the Somerset & Dorset in 1963 and without much effort worked local trains between Bath and Bournemouth.

In March 1965 *Evening Star* was withdrawn from Cardiff East Dock for official preservation after only five years service on BR. It was overhauled at Crewe in 1967, and stored for a short period before being loaned to the Keighley & Worth Valley Railway from July 1973 until May 1975. Now based at the National Railway Museum in York it makes periodic outings on the main line but was based at Minehead and used on the West Somerset Railway for the 1989 season.

The highlight of the North Yorkshire Moors Railway enthusiasts' weekend in October 1987, was the appearance of No. 92220 *Evening Star* from the National Railway Museum. On 11th October it did two return trips between Whitby and Goathland and one to Pickering. Despite the appearance of the single track in this picture, it is running on BR metals and has just passed Ruswarp heading its second train of the day from Whitby to Goathland.
John Whiteley

Evening Star arrives at Ribblehead station on the Settle and Carlisle line for a photographic stop and run past with the "Cumbrian Mountain Express" on 23rd April 1984.

Gavin Morrison

On 11th October 1987 No. 92220 departs from Whitby for the North Yorkshire Moors Railway.

John Whiteley

The "Border Venturer" special heads south over the Settle and Carlisle line near Langwathby headed by *Evening Star* on 13th May 1978.   *John Whiteley*

Heading back to Didcot it is leaving Banbury with the "Rising Star" tour on 13th September 1981.
                                                                                                 John Whiteley

The "Bishop Treacy" tour in memory of the famous railway photographer, is seen climbing past Horton-in-Ribblesdale on 30th September 1978 headed by No. 92220. *John Whiteley*

The "Border Venturer" special makes a spirited departure from Appleby behind *Evening Star* on 13th May 1978. *John Whiteley*

Evening Star blows off just at the right moment as it emerges from Pontrilas Tunnel with a return working of a "Welsh Marches Pullman" from Newport on 24th April 1982.

John Whiteley

End piece: No. 246 *Morayshire* heads west into the setting sun near Linlithgow with a special from Fife on 7th September 1980.
Gavin Morrison

Front endpaper: Different eras of GWR motive power are seen in this picture taken near Dorrington on 24th May 1986. *City of Truro* is piloting No. 6000 *King George V* on an excursion returning from Shrewsbury to Hereford.
John Whiteley

Rear endpaper: Having just passed Millom, Midland Compound 4-4-0 No. 1000 and 'Jubilee' class 4-6-0 No. 5690 *Leander* accelerate an excursion which originated in Southampton, towards its destination at Sellafield on 5th May 1980.
John Whiteley